"This book is a must for those who want to understand the Slovak people and how to interact with them more closely, to appreciate the uniqueness of Slovak culture, and to smooth the transition into Slovak life. It's an asset to the Slovak traveler's library."
—**Helene Cincebeaux, Founder and Director of Slovak Heritage & Folklore Society International**

"A great source of information on Slovakia. It provides not only the basics, but also answers questions that you would not normally consider or even think of."
—**František Hudák, Consul General of the Slovak Republic in Los Angeles**

"Resources that enable improvement in business communications for foreigners in Slovakia are important. This book is an asset for those who wish to get the most out of their stay."
—**Martin Krekáč, President of the Business Alliance of Slovakia**

"A very practical reference to the ins and outs of living in Slovakia and a great introduction to Slovakia's rich cultural heritage."
—**Elnora Rusnak, President of the Slovak Heritage Association of San Diego**

"A valuable book and a smart investment for those interested in preparing to live and work in Slovakia."
—**Vladimíra Josefiová, Director of Human Resources, VUB Banka**

THE FOREIGNER'S GUIDE TO LIVING IN

SLOVAKIA

MARGARETE HURN

MODRA PUBLISHING

Photographs by Ľubomír Báťa
Content edit by Peter Mráz
Illustrations by Margarete Hurn

ISBN: 978-0-979-0300-3-1
LCCN: 2006940671

Modra Publishing
www.modra-publishing.com
info@modra-publishing.com

Version 1.1

Dedication

To Igor for his confidence and support, and to our families.

Acknowledgements

Many people helped me by providing valuable feedback and advice on the numerous topics covered in this book. I wish to make special mention of the following people:
Victoria Jannetta, Peter Mráz, Henry Tritchka, Brenda Lee, Helene Cincebeaux, James Thomson, Dr. Susan Mikula, Erika Kojšová, Miriam Švedlárová, Vladimír Taliga, Rose Gabaeff, Renée Fürst, Lauren Pederson, Danusha Goska, Rebekah Klein-Pejšová, Julie Michutka, Vladimír Bohinc, Ellen Kovac, Judy Hopkins-Trujillo, Danica Brečková, Jarmila Archlebová, Zuzana Motešická, and Ivona and Jakub Demáček.

I also owe a special thank you to the photographer Ľubomír Báťa who went the extra mile, literally and figuratively, to capture a variety of wonderful images of Slovak life. Thanks, Botto.

CONTENTS

LIST OF TABLES

ICONS USED THROUGHOUT THIS BOOK

NOTE

An aside or comment, additional to the primary information within a chapter section.

ATTENTION

A caution about possible problems or a warning to proceed with care.

REMINDER

Information that you may want to remember.

SEE MORE

A reference to another section in the book or to an additional resource for further information.

Preface

Moving to a new country is rarely easy. There is much room for confusion, misunderstanding, and a mistrust of behavior that is not understood. I have experienced these feelings first-hand and appreciate the importance of acclimating to a new environment in as short a time as possible.

Seven years ago I arrived in central Slovakia, alone but excited, and also a bit apprehensive. I had a job teaching English in a town too small to be mentioned in any travel guide. Even though I spoke only a handful of words and didn't know anyone besides the school principal, I was bolstered by the fact that I had a place to live and Slovak currency in my wallet. I felt safe in the knowledge that I was in a European country with customs and traditions that would not be entirely "foreign", although they certainly would be different from those I had known in America.

As soon as I stepped out on the street I began to have doubts. I saw numerous people tending fruit and vegetable gardens on plots of land by the roadside. Was gardening simply a popular hobby or was it a necessity? Didn't grocery stores stock enough fresh foods? The grocery store was my next destination and when I located it, I discovered another mystery—a group of people standing in front of the turnstile waiting for something. Why didn't anyone walk through and begin shopping? What were they waiting for? I felt awkward not knowing what to do and realized within that short period of time that understanding Slovak culture wasn't going to be as simple as I thought it would be.

As time went by, and little by little I learned from my students and friends about daily life and how to go about fulfilling my goal of living as a productive member of my adopted society. It wasn't easy and some things took longer to adjust to than others, but my road to self-fulfillment was laden with discovery and an awareness that things can be done in different ways. Of course, before you take such a giant leap of faith, moving to another country, you hope to be as prepared as possible, to know what you are getting into, and to have an understanding of what you can expect. In the end, however, no matter how much you read, ask questions, and do research, you will still feel the 'culture shock' of entering an environment that is so very different from your own.

This book is primarily intended for people who are going to Slovakia for an extended period of time to work or study. Certainly, this book won't be able to answer all of your questions and concerns, but nonetheless, its purpose is to help guide your learning about Slovak history, culture, and life if you are not already familiar, and to encourage you to take that leap into something that could be one of the most rewarding experiences of your life.

Margarete Hurn
San Diego, California

Map of Slovakia

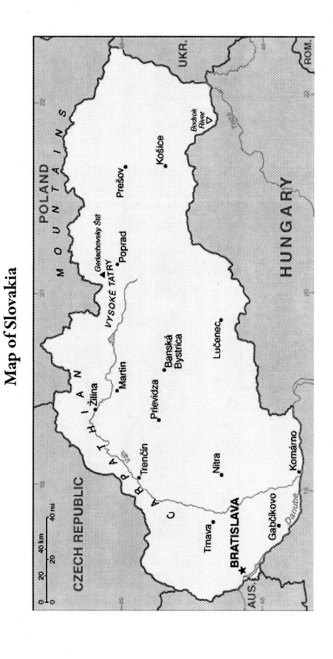

THE LAND AND ITS PEOPLE

When I first announced that I was moving to Slovakia to teach English, I heard lots of comments such as, "You're going where? To Czechoslovakia?" and "Oh, I had a grandmother who was from Slovenia." After I had patiently explained the location of Slovakia in Central Europe, the next question I often heard was "Why have you chosen to go there?" But the better question is "Why not?"

Slovakia is at the geographic center of Europe, and at the crossroads of European history and culture. It has seen Magyars, Turks, Nazis, and communists, and yet it has retained its identity: as a deeply religious, traditionally rural, proudly Slavic nation.

Slovakia has a population of 5.3 million, a number that most Slovaks consider to be woefully small. I'm always quick to remind them that Norway has a population of 4.4 million and has been able to successfully distinguish itself from other neighboring Scandinavian countries. Slovakia is distinguishing itself from other Slavic countries by highlighting its unique history, culture and language.

Slovakia and the other former Soviet satellite countries are no longer considered "Eastern Europe." Slovakia and many of its neighbors such as Poland, the

Czech Republic, and Hungary are often called "Central Europe." In fact, most Slovaks consider Slovakia to be the very center or "heart" of Europe. Several other countries also claim to be the center of Europe, however; depending on how geographic boundaries are defined.

NOTE

The correct adjective form is "Slovak" and not "Slovakian". For example, "Slovak people" or the "Slovak language."

NOTE

The country name "Slovakia" is the shortened form of the more formal "Slovak Republic." Both terms are used equally.

THE PHYSICAL ENVIRONMENT

Slovakia is 49,035 sq. km, or 8,921 sq. mi, and is comprised of a mostly rural environment. About 45 percent of the population lives in villages of fewer than 5,000 inhabitants, and 14 percent in villages of fewer than 1,000. The largest cities are the nation's capital of Bratislava with a population of approximately 447,000; Košice ('ko-shee-tse), located in east Slovakia at 242,000; and Prešov ('pre-sho), also located in east Slovakia at 94,000. Its neighboring countries are Austria to the west, the Czech Republic to the northwest, Poland to the north, Ukraine to the east, and Hungary to the south.

Depending on the area you travel through in Slovakia, you will see three kinds of topography: flat-lands, rolling hills, and mountains. In the south, the land is more consistently flat as it tapers down to the Danube river basin. Although agriculture is an important component throughout the entire country, the greatest variety of produce is grown in the fertile south. In the north, by contrast, it is hard to miss the impressive Tatra Mountains, which are by far the most distinguishable land feature in Slovakia.

Mountainous terrain is a major part of the nation's geography. Almost half of the country is taken up by the Carpathian arc; ranges include the High and Low Tatras, Small Fatra, and Big Fatra, the Slovak Ore Mountains, and the smaller ranges of the Lesser Carpathians and White Carpathians. The Slovak connection to nature is a direct result of these dramatic and beautiful mountains that stand as a national symbol. Three mountains are featured on the coat of arms and national flag, and are understood to represent the Matra, Fatra, and Tatra Mountains. The Matras are located in Hungary—Slovakia was once a part of Hungary—whereas the Fatra and Tatra ranges are in Slovakia. The Tatra Mountains, the nation's highest, are particularly important and mentioned in the first line of the Slovak National Anthem, "Lightning flashes over the Tatra, thunder pounds wildly."

Wheat fields in the Nitra region

Slovaks often take trips to the mountains to ski in the winter, stay at cottages through Christmas and the New Year, and hike in the spring and summer. They are immensely proud of *Gerlachovský štít* – or Gerlach's Peak—the highest peak in the Tatra Mountain Range and the highest point in Slovakia at 2,655 meters high, 8,711 feet. Slovaks are also very proud that the mountains play host to a varied number of international tourists from nearby: Czechs, Hungarians, Germans, and Poles, as well as increasingly more Ukrainians and Russians.

Slovaks overwhelmingly identify with the mountains. This tie to nature is also reflected by the fact that Slovaks have a surprising knowledge of horticulture. The names of trees and many kinds of plants, flowers and mushrooms are common knowledge. A foreigner coming to Slovakia probably won't need to know the difference between a *dub* – oak and a *buk* – beech tree—two common trees found in Slovakia, but it is good to know that the *lipa* – linden—is the national tree.

Slovakia contains vast forest areas that are ideal for hiking. There are also thousands of caves, some of which have national protection status and have been designated World Heritage Sites with the United Nations Educational, Scientific and Cultural Organization (UNESCO), which is an organization dedicated to the preservation and restoration of sites of historic or natural significance. A large number of natural springs can also be found throughout the country, many of which are thermal and contain high mineral content. Because of their chemical and physical properties, the waters from these springs have healing effects, contributing over hundreds of years to the steady interest in spa culture for treatment of various kinds of ailments.

Decades of environmental degradation under communist governments had left many parts of Central and Eastern Europe in poor condition. Since that time, the Slovak government has made progress in environmental areas, though reform has not come as quickly as some would like. Overall, awareness about the environment has increased, and meeting environmental requirements set by the European Union (EU) is a priority.

THE ECONOMY

Slovakia has made most of the difficult transition from a centrally planned economy to a market economy, with privatization nearly complete. Currently, Slovakia is in the midst of an ambitious economic reform process intended to encourage rapid growth in productivity, increase the lagging employment rate, and raise the per-capita income levels to be economically in line with more advanced EU nations.[1] The kinds of reforms that have been implemented include the following:

- comprehensive tax reform of personal and income tax, and on value-added tax (VAT)
- massive cuts to previously generous welfare benefits for the long-term unemployed
- increasing the retirement age and making pension benefits dependent on work and contribution history

Reforms such as these and an improved business environment are some of the main reasons for a sharp increase in foreign direct investment (FDI), particularly from the automobile industry. Another reason for the growth spurt may be Slovakia's accession into the EU and other western organizations like NATO and the Organisation for Economic Co-operation and Development (OECD), which also serve to

1.   Policy Report of the OECD "Economic Survey of the Slovak Republic, 2005", p. 1

assure potential investors that Slovakia is politically and economically stable. Additionally, Slovakia attracts new investors for a number of reasons[1]:

- an inexpensive and skilled labor force

- geographic location close to western European markets

- reasonably developed infrastructure, particularly in the western portion of the country

The National Bank of Slovakia (NBS)

1.   According to Zdenko Štefanides, senior analyst with VÚB Bank, as cited in the Slovak Spectator 9/6/2004

The Bratislava region continues to see the overwhelming majority of foreign investment with its developed infrastructure and more qualified workforce. However, this strong investment in the capital further widens the gap between the wealthier western part of the country and the poorer, less developed east. The government is trying to address this disparity by offering more incentives to investors if they go to other regions, such as offering longer tax breaks, but so far this approach has only been partly successful.

Unemployment figures in the year 2006 clearly demonstrate this division between the eastern and western regions of the country. In Bratislava, unemployment remained below five percent in 2006, whereas, according to the OECD, unemployment for all of Slovakia stood at 13.5 percent in 2006.

Slovakia's future includes the following challenges:

- develop ways in which to increase employment

- meet the necessary requirements to adopt the euro currency in 2009

- continue reforms to cut waste and make the government more effective

While Slovaks know the path to economic stability won't come easily, generally the people are willing to make sacrifices for a brighter future. This doesn't mean their patience is limitless. Slovaks want to see the results of reform in the near term, and depending on how these successes develop, sentiment can change accordingly. This was demonstrated in the last general election in June 2006, when the ruling coalition that had implemented many reforms was ousted from power.

THE LANGUAGE

Slovaks have their own language. The Slovak language has its roots in Slavonic, which played an important role in all Slavic languages, such as Russian or Ukrainian (much the way Latin influenced the Romance languages). Slovak, like Czech and Polish, belongs to the branch of Western Slavic languages. Is it possible for a person who speaks Slovak to understand someone speaking Polish? Well, yes and no. It's possible to get the gist of things, but the details will remain sketchy.

It is, however, possible for Czechs and Slovaks to understand one another, as their languages are more similar. The mutual intelligibility of Czech and Slovak was mainly advanced when the nations were united under Czechoslovakia. Such a union made TV programs, radio, films, books, and other materials of both languages widely available. The exchange wasn't exactly balanced, however, as the majority of compositions, from official government documents to film and literature, was produced only in Czech. This has worked to the benefit of Slovaks—a lifetime of exposure to the Czech language, from cartoons to university textbooks, has allowed for many Slovaks to develop Czech language skills to near native-speaker levels. The ability of Czechs and Slovaks to understand each other's language is likely to change, however. Young Czechs and Slovaks (born after 1993) will not have the same exposure and, therefore, the ability to communicate in each other's language may be significantly reduced.

There are other languages spoken in Slovakia, though they aren't as common. In north east Slovakia, closest to the the Ukrainian border, Rusyn (an Eastern-Slavic language closer to Ukrainian and Belarusian) is spoken. Additionally, along the northern border with Poland, it's possible to hear Polish spoken. Hungarian is spoken in many of the villages and smaller towns in the south and along the south east border. Slovaks of Hungarian descent make up the largest ethnic minority in the country, at approximately ten percent. This population is sizable enough that the issue of whether the Hungarian language should be spoken in schools or used for public and administrative purposes is still a topic of debate.

A village sign in both Slovak and Hungarian

Since the fall of the Iron Curtain, English has become a popular language to study for many students. English and German are the languages most often taught to Slovak K-12 students. University students also have foreign language requirements and many opt to study English. People in their 40s or older, who grew up under communist rule, had few opportunities to study English, and instead studied and spoke Russian. When visiting a Slovak family at home, it is common for the teenage son or daughter to serve as the translator between his or her parents and visiting English-speaking guests. Despite many Slovaks' ability to speak two or three languages, quickly finding an English translator to help out in a jam can prove difficult. English isn't as common as in other western countries like Germany or Sweden, where almost everyone speaks 'a little' English. If you need an English speaker's help, look for people who look like university students or young professionals.

If you have never studied a Slavic language before, you might find learning Slovak a real challenge. Don't let this put you off. It is rewarding to know a few basic phrases when starting out. Even if you are traveling with someone who can translate everything for you, the locals appreciate the personal effort you make to communicate. Slovaks themselves consider their language to be difficult, so they value any effort from a foreigner trying to speak in Slovak.

To give you some idea of the major differences that exist between the Slavic family of languages and English, consider the following examples: first, nouns change form depending on their grammatical relation to other words in the sentence. Notice how the word *káva* (coffee) changes in the sentences below:

Table 1: Language differences between Slovak and English

I don't want coffee.	Nechcem *kávu*.
I drink milk with coffee.	Pijem mlieko s *kávou*.
Add sugar to the coffee.	Pridaj cukor do *kávy*.

Second, verbs indicate grammatical person by changing form. For example, notice the endings on the following conjugated verb:

hovoriť - to speak			
hovorím	I speak	hovoríme	we speak
hovoríš	you speak	hovoríte	you speak
hovorí	he/she speaks	hovoria	they speak

For anyone who is planning to stay for an extended period of time, learning the language is advisable—the more you know, the more you feel a part of things. And the Slovaks have a great expression, *Koľko rečí vieš, toľkokrát si človekom*, which translated literally means: "The more languages you know, the more times you are a human being." Put another way, the more languages you speak, the better able you are to see things from different cultural perspectives.

If you aren't going to live in a larger city that has institutions that teach Slovak, a personal tutor is an excellent alternative. There are many teachers and educated individuals capable of teaching Slovak and would appreciate the experience of teaching an English speaker their language.

Here are a few names and addresses of institutions that teach Slovak to foreigners:

Table 2: Slovak language study for foreigners

Akadémia vzdelávania (37 locations throughout Slovakia) Centrum jazykov Gorkého 10 815 17 Bratislava +421 (0)2 5441 0225 www.aveducation.sk	ACE- Assured Communication in English Nerudova 14 040 01 Košice +421 (0)55 622 7981 www.ace-sro.sk
Caledonian School Obchodná 35 811 07 Bratislava +421 (0)2 5293 2645 www.caledonainschool.sk	Canadian Bilingual Institute Obchodná 43-49 811 06 Bratislava +421 (0)2 5292 2384 www.cbi.sk
Comenius University Institute for Languages Šoltésovej 4 811 08 Bratislava +421 (0)2 5557 7333 www.uniba.sk/ujop	

Find a more extensive list of schools in *The Slovak Spectator's* "Book of Lists," a resource guide containing the contact information for companies and organizations operating in Slovakia. Information ranges from a listing of Internet service providers and consulting firms to moving companies and language schools. The Internet version of this resource is called the "Green Pages" and is located at www.greenpages.sk.

See Appendix C for basic words and expressions in Slovak.

SEE MORE

RELIGION

Slovakia can be described as a religious nation. According to the census provided by the Statistical Office of the Slovak Republic in 2001, 87 percent of the people are affiliated with some kind of religion. Roman Catholics comprise the majority with more than 68 percent of the total population. Church attendance is strong, and in the towns and villages, it isn't uncommon to see parishioners at Sunday mass standing outside the church doors because of lack of space inside.

The country has a long religious history that includes the figures who spread Christianity to the Slavic people— Saints Cyril and Methodius. They were invited to Great Moravia (an area that included western Slovakia in the ninth century and of which Nitra was an important principality) on a mission to spread Christianity in the language of the Slavic people. With the use of the Glagolitic alphabet that Cyril had created, the two brothers were the first to translate the Bible and other books into the newly written Slavic language. Religion was a powerful tool in those times and the initial purpose was to make the Moravian Empire independent from the powerful Frankish Empire. More importantly, however, the creation and use of the Glagolitic alphabet marked the beginning of when the Slavic people began to lay the foundations for their own culture. July 5 marks an important holiday in both Slovakia and the Czech Republic, to honor Saints Cyril and Methodius.

According to stories, Saints Cyril and Methodius brought the symbol of the double-bar cross to Slovakia. The double-bar cross, which is featured prominently on the Slovak coat of arms and in the national flag, was once a symbol used by the Byzantine Empire. Today some people interpret the double-bar cross on Slovak emblems as a representation of Slovaks as guardians of the Christian tradition.

Easter Monday in the village of Olšavica near Levoča

In addition to Roman Catholicism, Protestantism, Byzantine Catholicism (also called Greek Catholicism but not to be confused with Greek Orthodoxy), Reformist Christianity, and Judaism are represented in Slovakia. Under communist rule, all forms of religious worship were strongly suppressed. Though not strictly forbidden, religious practice was strongly discouraged through institutionalized demotion at work, denial of university education for one's children, loss of property, or imprisonment. Along with purges of clergy, strict controls for ordaining new clergy, the confiscation or destruction of religious property, the censoring of printed religious matter, and the outlawing of religious instruction to children, persecution drove religious practice underground.

As with many Central European countries, the Jewish community of today is a fraction of what it had been formerly. Today there are roughly 2,300 Jews in Slovakia with the majority in the larger cities of Bratislava and Košice, and in a few larger towns. Bratislava has the most significant population of Jews in the country. With more than 800 years of history, it is considered one of the major centers of European Judaism.

The most significant Jewish site is the mausoleum containing the tomb of Chatam Sofer, the greatest Jewish scholar of the nineteenth century. The mausoleum, which contains the graves of not only Chatam Sofer but also other important rabbis, is located below ground, a few feet from a tram line under the Bratislava castle. The grave was located in a portion of the Jewish cemetery in Bratislava that was confiscated in 1943 to build a roadway. [1]

SEE MORE For more information on the history of Jews in Slovakia, see "Germans and Jews in Slovak History" on page 34.

1.   Today visitors to the memorial must make an appointment with the Jewish Religious Community of Bratislava prior to arriving (+421 (0)2 5441 2167).

Finally, an interesting point to note is that in the Czech Republic, the number of people who practice any kind of religion is significantly lower than in Slovakia; the Czech Republic's population is 40 percent atheist and 39 percent Roman Catholic. This is just one example to demonstrate that, although the Czech and Slovak Republics share some history and culture, they also retain differences.

ETHNIC GROUPS

According to the Statistical Office of the Slovak Republic in 2002, ethnic populations in Slovakia broke down as follows: Slovak 85.8%, Hungarian 9.7%, Roma 1.7%, Czech 0.8%, and Rusyn, Ukrainian, Russian, German, Polish and others 2%. Though ethnic Slovaks make up the clear majority, issues regarding ethnic minorities are frequently in the news and common topics for discussion and debate.

THE HUNGARIANS

An issue of contention involves the Hungarian minority and how far their rights extend as a protected ethnic group in Slovakia. According to the Statistical Office of the Slovak Republic in 2001, the Hungarian population in Slovakia numbers approximately 520,000 and is mainly clustered in the southern part of the country, along the border with Hungary. Before 1918, the group of Hungarians living on present day Slovak soil was still living within the political borders of their Hungarian homeland. This changed after the dissolution of the Austro-Hungarian Empire after World War I, and new borders were drawn to create independent countries such as Czechoslovakia. The birth of Czechoslovakia meant the end of Slovaks living on territory of the Hungarian Kingdom. It also meant that roles were reversed to some extent: Slovaks would be part of their own nation state while a Hungarian minority would be located within the Czechoslovak borders.

Many ethnic Slovaks view the country's historical tie with Hungary negatively—the role of oppressor for a thousand years. Some Slovaks mistrust ethnic Hungarians whom they view as not having made an attempt to integrate into Slovak society through the use of the Slovak language. In 2003, a law was passed establishing a Hungarian university in Southern Slovakia, creating protest and irritation from Slovaks fearful that a Hungarian dominance or "magyarization" of the south would take place if measures were not put in place to stop it.

Ultimately some Slovaks fear that the Hungarian minority will attempt to gain autonomy from Slovakia, and the Hungarian nation will use the ethnic minority to gain a foothold to expand Hungarian influence. To a great extent this fear is exaggerated, but when the parliament in Hungary passed a status law in 2001 extending special benefits to ethnic Hungarians living in the countries bordering Hungary, it sparked widespread political and social debate. Two years later both countries signed a bilateral agreement, bringing this particular issue to an end.

A sign for a secondary-grammar school in Slovak and Hungarian

Today debate continues on the use of the Hungarian language in the public sphere and in education, and bilingual signs in areas with a larger Hungarian population. Though there were some setbacks in minority rights in the few years after Slovakia became an independent nation in 1993, there has been progress. The passage of a law on minority language use and EU membership obligations have encouraged the Slovak government to adopt additional laws supporting minority rights. Also, the Hungarian Coalition Party, the largest Hungarian party in Slovakia, has been a solid part of the Slovak governing coalitions in past governments. Their objectives have been to strengthen the Hungarian community within Slovak society and promote the rights of minority groups in Slovakia.

THE ROMA

The Roma (also called "Gypsies," though this term can be interpreted at derogatory) are the second largest minority after the Hungarian community, at approximately 320,000. This number, the result of a survey that was conducted on behalf of the Slovak Cabinet in 2004, is in sharp contrast to the results of the national census in 2001 that previously estimated the Roma population at 90,000. Since it is possible to choose only one ethnicity in a census, a likely explanation of the disparity between these two estimations is that in the last major census many Roma may have identified them-selves as being of a different ethnicity other than Roma. Slovakia is considered to have a large Roma minority in comparison to other EU nations.

According to a study conducted by the United Nations Development Programme (UNDP), the Roma are socially marginalized. An increasing number of Roma live in isolated settlements with poor or no access to basic utilities such as running water, electricity, sanitation, sewage, waste removal, and transportation. All in all, the Roma are at a disadvantage compared to the majority population in education, housing, employment, and health care.

Also according to the UNDP, the unemployment rate among the Roma population in 2003 was approximately 64 percent. The main reasons cited were a combination of discriminatory practices in hiring, economic depression in the country, and limited education and job skills of the Roma population.[1] Due to poverty and high unemployment, many Roma are dependent on social welfare that in the past had been generous to the long-term unemployed.

Another problem that the Roma face is that of negative stereotyping. Attitudes like, "the Roma abuse the social system and refuse to work or send their children to school" persist. Additionally, the majority population doesn't identify with Roma culture and/or societal norms, particularly because Roma culture is at times contrary to values of the surrounding culture, and there is a great deal of intolerance. In an interview with The Slovak Spectator, Slovak Cabinet representative for the Roma Community, Klára Orgovánová said that much has been done to improve the perception of the Roma in the last several years, but that "much of this has been accomplished only due to pressure from international institutions and because Slovakia has had to climb to a certain standard".[2]

Though outside pressure has been a source of encouragement, it has also created negative generalizations about the Slovak government and people by spotlighting the appalling conditions of the Roma and the government's perceived lack of progress on tackling the issue. A few western media outlets, particularly tabloid newspapers, have

1. For more information on issues relating to unemployment, see UNDP RSC staff 2003: Chapter 3, "Avoiding the Dependency Trap."
2. The Slovak Spectator; "Slovaks Begin to Discuss Racial Discrimination." Volume 10, No. 28, July 19-25, 2004

come to Slovakia to take pictures of Roma children playing in mud puddles with sensationalist stories of how Slovak Gypsies are on their way to Western Europe to become the burden of wealthier EU counties. This has not proved to be the case so far. The attention has generally made Slovaks bitter about how their country is portrayed internationally. They are even more certain that a person with no first-hand experience of the Roma situation in Slovakia can truly understand the entire scope of concerns beyond an interview and some photographs.

Roma children from the village of Malé Chrášťany

Without a doubt the topic is very complex, and there are numerous opinions as to the exact nature of the problem and how it should be solved. On the one hand, the plight of the Roma is an important social issue that demands continued attention to improve and resolve conditions. On the other hand, the Slovak majority is sensitive to being labeled racists or thought of as disinterested in finding a solution to the issue. If you are ever in a pub having a drink with some Slovaks and looking for something to chat about, the subject of the Roma in Slovakia is one that is best left untouched.

BLOCKS OF FLATS

You can't escape them. They're everywhere. From Bratislava to the small towns deep in the countryside, the unmistakably utilitarian, communist architecture stands out as a glaring eyesore. If you are traveling from Vienna to Bratislava you can't miss the clustered blocks in the distance, looking quite formidable (they're not that inspiring up close). The view from Bratislava castle looking over the Danube to the blocks in Petržalka, the most densely populated area of Bratislava, is quite amazing.

They were built beginning in the 1960s as the answer to a housing shortage. Slovakia, as many other communist countries, went through a period of rapid, and sometimes forceful, industrialization after World War II, especially in the 1960s and 1970s. Industrial areas were mostly concentrated in larger towns and cities, which meant that many people were moving from rural to urban areas for work. In predominantly agrarian societies such as Slovakia before 1918, and to some extent even before World War II, this had a major impact on urban development and the housing market. The government needed to build urban housing for thousands of people, and they needed to build them fast. Blocks of flats were considered to be the most effective option, the aesthetics aside. They also strengthened the feeling of community among the "working class."

While the 1970s saw the greatest numbers of blocks built, massive construction continued throughout Slovakia and many other satellite countries into the 1980s. A *činžák*, or *panelák*—as they are built of concrete "panels"—have little to distinguish themselves from one another and are often considered quite ugly. Don't let that fool you into thinking that these structures reflect the same characteristics inside.

Families often take great care in the style, function, and individuality of their home. This is no different in a block apartment. In most friends' flats that I have visited, I have been impressed with the atmosphere of comfort and cheerfulness, in stark contrast to the hallways, stairwells, and public areas of blocks that tend to be dark and depressing. Having lived in one of these flats myself, I can attest that the heating and insulation are more than acceptable and, in the smaller towns, they tend to be more conveniently located closer to the center of town.

A common sight across all of Slovakia and former communist countries in Central and Eastern Europe

In addition to their unsightliness and the fact that you can easily confuse your address for another, the greatest negative for me is that once a year, usually in the summer, the hot water is turned off for a period lasting from three days to a week. The reason why? Because the heating system assigned to various blocks of flats has to undergo general maintenance. The first time I was faced with this occurrence, I panicked as to how I would last the week with cold showers. But after I began boiling the first pot of water for a bath, I got over it.

THE SLOVAK GARDENER

I lived in a block of flats on the outskirts of a small town, in which the view from my kitchen balcony was a huge flat field divided into small lots. On these small lots, families grew their gardens. From my balcony I watched people spend their weekends working the soil, tilling, planting, cleaning, and picking, from sun up to sun down. Gardens are almost always used for growing fruits and vegetables, though a few flowers and grass are added to please the eye.

A typical garden in Slovakia often has potatoes, carrots, and onions as well as various fruit trees, and perhaps some grapevines.

Gardening is more than just a simple hobby to pass the time; it is a way of life that includes the preserving and processing of many items of produce such as berry jams and preserves, pickled gherkins and sauerkraut, and grapes for wine or fruits for stronger spirits. People are proud of their gardens, and rightly so. More often they are generous and pleased to share some jars of whatever you might fancy, or whatever Grandma thinks you should have stocked at home.

Since the time I first witnessed people working on their plots of land, I have learned that many Slovaks go to great lengths to access land where they can grow fruits and vegetables, even if it is inconveniently located (sometimes kilometers) from their homes. Why is gardening so important? The answer is in Slovak roots, leftover from the village lifestyle. As mentioned previously, Slovakia didn't become truly industrialized until after World War II, under socialist Czechoslovakia. Until that time Slovakia was almost entirely rural. For this reason, Slovaks typically have a strong relationship with nature and still feel the lure to work the land for themselves.

Though gardening is important to many Slovaks, there are families, particularly in the larger cities, who have given it up or chosen not to have the responsibility of a garden because of time constraints or lack of interest. Certainly you couldn't save such a substantial amount of money growing your own produce to make gardening a necessity. Life in the fast-paced world makes time more of a commodity; a garden with all of its responsibilities has the potential to become a symbol of stress rather than a nerve soother. Regardless, it is easy enough to be in contact with someone who would be happy to give you a few jars for your pantry and for you to use in your next cherry-filled *štrúdľa*.

ICE-HOCKEY (THE SECOND RELIGION)

Every year, beginning on the last Saturday in April, World Championship hockey descends over the nation like a long anticipated summer vacation. People begin to talk about the championship weeks in advance, parties are planned, and preparations made to make the most of the three-week roller coaster ride of quick action and high suspense.

The Slovak National Hockey Team, which qualifies for the World Championships every year, is made up of a group of spirited professional athletes—many of them are professional NHL players—but are considered to be local boys by Slovaks. They are an inspiration to the young and old, male and female alike.

Courtesy of Tony Frič

SNP Square in Bratislava after the victory in 2002

In 2002, the Slovak National Team made history when they won the gold medal for the first time since Slovak independence. Following the win was 24 hours of nation-wide, non-stop celebration not seen since the anti-communist revolution. The win was especially significant because it allowed the country to unite in the belief that not only could it participate in the global arena but it could have confidence in its competitive role world-wide. The championship has become a symbol of Slovak potential. The dream to be able to chant *My sme majstri* – We are the champions—is enough to bring hope alive year after year.

If you are lucky enough to be in Slovakia during these weeks in April and May, don't miss the opportunity to catch a game, preferably where you are surrounded by other Slovaks (everyone will know when the next game is scheduled) and get ready to be swept along in the frenzy. You don't have to be a die-hard hockey fan to enjoy the show, and it's quite easy to get caught up in excitement when it's almost tangible enough to touch.

The relationship between people and nature is strong, even in modern-day Slovakia.

SLOVAK IDENTITY AND INFLUENCE
THROUGH HISTORY

It is fair to say that history is controversial; Slovak history is no exception. In Slovakia, several historic events have been interpreted in more than one way and are subject to debate even today. Every effort has been made to make this brief overview of Slovak history as unbiased as possible. A list of consulted resources is included at the end of the chapter.

The issue of national identity can be an emotional point with many Slovaks. Generally, they see themselves as a proud people whose ancestors have been under the thumb of other nations for more than a thousand years. If you consider that the first opportunity for Slovakia to function under its own independent government came in 1939, which is fairly recent compared to the dates of independence for many other European nations, you will begin to understand that the struggle for independence is still considered fresh for many Slovaks. The country had its first, brief period of independence in the years during World War II. The present period began less than 15 years ago; thus, Slovakia is one of the newest countries in the world.

From the Beginning

People have inhabited the land between the Carpathians and the Danube River for thousands of years. The Celts entered the region in the fifth century B.C. and built large settlements in the areas around Bratislava and Liptov. Around the birth of Christ, the Roman Empire spread to the Danube where outposts were established and maintained. Remnants of both cultures can still be found today in Slovakia. For example, the site of Devín Castle in Bratislava was settled by both the Celts and Romans, though at separate times, due to its strategic location at the confluence of the Danube and Morava Rivers.

NOTE

A legion of Roman soldiers left an inscription in a rock on Trenčín castle dated from around 179 AD. The inscription is believed to be proof of one of the northern-most borders of the Roman Empire.

Slavs came to the territory of present-day Slovakia in the fifth century. The origin of the Slavs is debated but they most probably came from an area in Eastern Europe. They settled in east, central, and south Europe, mixing with existing local populations. Slavs are divided along linguistic lines; thus, there are southern Slavs (for example, Bulgarians, Serbs, Croats), western Slavs (Czechs, Slovaks, and Poles), and eastern Slavs (Russians, Ukrainians, and Belarusians).

The first important state organization of the western Slavs was the Empire of Samo, which was established in the seventh century. In the ninth century, Old Slovakia, or "territorium Nitriense" as it was chronicled, was a vital part of the Great Moravian Empire from which kings and princes such as Mojmír, Pribina, and Svätopluk have earned a place in Slovak legend. The empire encompassed the lands of present-day Slovakia and Moravia, and parts of Hungary, Austria, Bohemia, and southern Poland. The Great

Moravian Empire lasted less than a century but maintains a strong legacy for two important reasons: rapid cultural development of the Slavs, and the catalyst for Christianity to gain a foothold in Central Europe.

In 863 A.D., two brothers Constantine (later called Cyril) and Methodius were dispatched from the Byzantine Empire to the Great Moravian Empire. They were sent for by Rastislav, king of the Great Moravian Empire, who wanted to limit Frankish influence (the Franks were a Germanic people), and desired that his people be evangelized in their own Slavic language. Constantine and Methodius, who are celebrated saints today, created the Glagolitic alphabet, which later became the basis for the Cyrillic alphabet, and translated several religious works, including the Bible, into the ancient Slavonic language.

In 868 A.D., Pope Adrian II confirmed the Slavonic language as the fourth liturgical language along with Latin, Greek, and Hebrew.

NOTE

See the section "Religion" on page 12 for more information on Saints Cyril and Methodius.

SEE MORE

THE HUNGARIAN FACTOR

For a period of roughly a thousand years, the land that formed the core of present day Slovakia had been under the dominance of the Hungarian Kingdom, a fact that will forever remain in the Slovak psyche. If you were to comment that some present-day Hungarians still experience pangs of regret from losing 70 percent of their territory (including Slovakia) after World War I, you wouldn't likely get any sympathy from a Slovak, but rather a sharp-toned retort that it wasn't soon enough nor was it entirely Hungarian land to begin with.

Conflict began at the end of the ninth century when the Slavs of the Danube Basin, already worn down by their battles with the Franks, were threatened by the aggression of the Huns (the Huns were a semi-nomadic tribe who lived in present-day Hungary). The Moravian Empire came to an end, and the region that is Slovakia today was integrated into the developing Hungarian Kingdom. From the tenth century until the twentieth century the history of Slovakia was entwined with the Hungarian Kingdom, shifting under the push and pull of battles between the Hungarians and other neighboring sovereign nations.

THE AUSTRIAN FACTOR

In 1526 the Hungarian armies collapsed under the strain of the Turkish invasion, resulting in the partitioning of the Hungarian Kingdom into three parts. The region in the northwest, which was made up of Slovakia, parts of present-day Croatia, western Hungary and Burgenland (present-day eastern Austria), was annexed by Austria and called *Royal Hungary*. Since the advance of the Ottoman Empire had resulted in the shifting of national boundaries, this north-western region became the center of the Hungarian principality with Bratislava (known as *Pressburg* in German, *Pozsony* in Hungarian, and *Prešporok* in Slovak) as its capital, the meeting place of the Hungarian Diet, and the coronation town for Hungarian Kings (i.e., the ruling family of the Habsburgs). From 1526 to 1830, 19 Habsburg sovereigns were crowned as kings and queens of Hungary in St. Martin's Cathedral, located in present-day Old Town Bratislava.

NOTE

Instead of a cross that is typically found at the top of a church spire, a gold crown is seen on the spire of St. Martin's Cathedral, a reminder of its historic importance.

While the Habsburgs were emperors and empresses of Austria and ruled from the capital in Vienna, they were also called "kings and queens of Hungary." The Slovaks didn't fare much better under the Habsburg umbrella, as the principal battles to defend the Habsburg Empire against the Ottoman Turks were fought on Slovak soil, exacting a high death toll. Also, with the all-consuming costs of war, Slovakia's rich resources of silver and gold were all but depleted. Up until the Turkish expansion, Slovakia was the biggest silver producer and the second largest gold producer in Europe.

THE AUSTRO-HUNGARIAN FACTOR

In the mid-nineteenth century, a wave of nationalism swept across Europe, bringing inspiration and enlightenment to, among others, the suppressed minorities of multinational states. Up until 1842, Latin had been used as the language of administration throughout the lands under Habsburg jurisdiction. The Latin language, perhaps because it wasn't a language associated with any specific ethnicity, served as a unifying factor that held everything together. But when the Habsburgs renewed their attempts to centralize the Empire through the German language, the Hungarian parliament followed suit and replaced Latin with Magyar in Hungarian lands, and thus began the era of "Magyarization"—policies that forced the acceptance of the Hungarian language and culture on to non-ethnic Hungarians in Hungarian-ruled regions. This was one of the catalysts that pushed men such as Ľudovít Štúr, Michal Miloslav Hodža, and Jozef Miloslav Hurban to become leaders of a movement to promote Slovak identity, a movement now known as the "National Awakening."

The most prominent Slovak figure of this time is Ľudovít Štúr, who is credited with the work of standardizing the Slovak language and its written form in 1846. The standardized language, which was based on the Central Slovak dialect, gained wide acceptance after a few years and spurred a wave of Slovak literature that helped shape national identity. All of that would have to be put on hold, however, as in 1848, known as the "year of revolutions," the Hungarians attempted to declare their independence, which resulted in the Austrians putting down the revolt with military force. Štúr and others had seized upon these events to demand equal status for Slovaks in the monarchy, but it never materialized and Habsburg rule was reinstated.

The shift to the more balanced, dual monarchy of the Austro-Hungarian Empire was born in 1867 as a result of a compromise between the Habsburg monarchy of Austria and the Hungarian nobility. The union between these two parties was necessary to preserve the Habsburg Empire, which had been weakened by battles against the Prussians and Italians, and to compromise with the Hungarian Kingdom to remain unified under one monarchy. The compromise came by loosening the hold of Austrian control from Vienna and by allowing Hungary to restore its constitution and establish a parliament with the powers to enact its own laws.

The Kingdom of Hungary in 1876

Present-day Slovakia

Present-day Hungary

For Slovaks this turn of events was catastrophic. Where previously direct rule from Vienna had kept Hungarian might at bay, now the Hungarian government had direct jurisdiction over Slovak lands once again. The Hungarians received the rights and independence they had demanded from Austria but were quick to deny these very same rights to other nationalities living in the Hungarian Kingdom. Instead, the Hungarian Parliament passed acts that imposed more extensive Magyarization throughout Slovakia and the kingdom.

The years from the mid-nineteenth century until the outbreak of World War I in 1914 were very dark times in Slovak history. In 1907 the Hungarian authorities used their right to make Hungarian the sole language taught and spoken in primary and secondary schools. In addition to the steady progression of Magyarization, there was a drain of Slovaks who were emigrating in great numbers. By 1914 an estimated 20 percent of the total population on Slovak lands had left. Due to social and political oppression and the widespread poverty and malnutrition on Slovak lands, many Slovaks headed for Vienna or Budapest, but most were destined for North America.

In the United States, many Slovaks settled in Pennsylvania and Ohio with Pittsburgh becoming a major center for American Slovaks, mainly due to the mining and steel works that could employ many unskilled workers. By far the greatest number of Slovaks came from east and north Slovakia. It is said today that almost every family in east Slovakia can claim a relative or descendant in North America.

GERMANS AND JEWS IN SLOVAK HISTORY

The settlement of "Germans"—the term "Germans" refers more broadly to German speakers from the regions of Germany and Austria—in Slovakia took place over many centuries, beginning around the 12th century. Hungarian kings encouraged Germans to settle in towns that required skilled craftsmen, miners, and vintners. These Germans who lived on Slovak land, and continue to live there today, are referred to as "Carpathian Germans."

Throughout the Middle Ages, Germans played an important role in the development of towns in Slovakia, mainly in the three regions of Bratislava, Spiš, and Banská Bystrica; the latter two areas being important mining regions. Though most major towns and villages in Slovakia have a registered German (and Hungarian) name, there are still a few villages that are called exclusively by their German names today, such as the village of Limbach located outside of Bratislava.

Numbers of German populations in Slovakia illustrate an interesting point of just who were the minorities at different points in history. For example, consider the following two statistics:

- In 1880, the population of *Pressburg* – the German name for Bratislava, and its Hungarian name *Pozsony*, was as follows: Germans (68%), Slovaks (8%), Hungarians (8%).

- In 1921, the results of the first national census of Czechoslovakia were as follows: Czechs (50%), Germans (23%), Slovaks (14%), Hungarians (5.6%), Rusyns (3%), Jews (1%), Poles (.6%).

In 1938, there were about 140,000 Carpathian Germans in Slovakia. During World War II when the Red Army was approaching Slovakia, the majority of Germans were evacuated out of Slovakia. After the war ended, most Germans who remained were expelled. According to more recent census results from the beginning of the twentieth century, there are fewer than 6,000 Germans living in Slovakia.

Though there is evidence of Jewish settlements on the land of present-day Slovakia since the eleventh century, the most significant wave of migration of the Jewish population to Slovakia took place during the eighteenth and nineteenth centuries. Similar to the settlement of Carpathian Germans, Jews were also encouraged by the Hungarian rulers to settle in Upper Hungary—the Slovak lands that comprised the northern-most boundary of the Hungarian Kingdom until 1918.

Ethnologically, the concept of "Slovak Jews" is probably better defined as Jews of Upper Hungary until 1918, and then Jews in the territory of Slovakia, in Czechoslovakia, until 1993. Until 1918, Jews that lived in the Slovak lands in Upper Hungary were more closely associated with the Hungarian Kingdom.

Socially, Jews who settled in Slovak lands maintained their connections with Jewish communities in Bohemia and Moravia but also with communities in other parts of the Hungarian Kingdom. Politically, Hungarian officials supported Jewish cooperation in industry and finance.

Because of this association with the Hungarian Kingdom and the connection to commerce, and in part because of the characteristics that defined Jewish people— their practice of the Jewish faith, communication in their own language (most spoke German, Jewish-German, or Yiddish, though they learned the local language), and maintaining tight communities and social networks with other Jewish communities—a general sense of mistrust existed between the Jewish people and local Slovak populations.

Slovak-Jewish identity developed tentatively. In the time that is now referred to as the Age of Nationalism (1848-1914), the roots of national identities were just beginning to develop. During this time, Slovakia was not yet recognized as an independent nation; thus, Jews would not have had the ability or the inclination to identify themselves as Slovaks.

This development of Slovak-Jewish identity did expand with the birth of Czechoslovakia, particularly up until World War II. After the dissolution of the Austro-Hungarian Empire with the end of World War I, the Jews along with all the other ethnic groups gained legal protection as national groups within the newly created countries. Their rights were gradually taken away with the rise of anti-Semitism across Europe, and concluded with the violent expulsion and death of many thousands of Jews from Slovakia.

Examining the demographics of Jews in Slovakia just prior to the Second World War demonstrates the size of the Jewish population and also how they identified themselves according to nationality. On November 4, 1938, the daily-Slovak newspaper *Slovenský denník* published an article about Jews in Slovakia. The article included the following statistical data taken from 1930:

- 136,737 Jews lived in Slovakia and 102,542 in Subcarpathian Rus, which was more than 4% of the population in Slovakia and more than 14% of the population in Subcarpathian Rus.
- In Slovakia, 44,019 Jews declared Czech and Slovak nationality, 11,997 German nationality, and 72,644 Jewish nationality.

According to Livia Rothkirchen, a leading historian on Czech and Slovak Jewry, only about 25,000 of the pre-war Jewish population survived the Holocaust and of those, the majority of them left Slovakia after the war, most heading to Israel.

Today there are approximately 2,300 Jews living in Slovakia; the majority living in Bratislava and Košice. Though many symbols of Jewish life were destroyed or damaged in the Second World War and under the communist regime, there are approximately 200 synagogues and 620 Jewish cemeteries across Slovakia.

For more information on the most significant Jewish site in Slovakia, see the section on "Religion" on page 12.

SEE MORE

THE YEARS AS CZECHOSLOVAKIA

Slovakia was part of Czechoslovakia for more than 60 years (1918-1939; 1945-1992). After the end of World War I the incorporation of Czechs and Slovaks into one country seemed like a logical step. The idea had been developing by the end of the nineteenth century, when Czech and Slovak intellectuals, who were increasingly in contact with one another, found they could easily draw parallels between their cultures. Just as the Slovaks had been subjects under the Hungarians, the Czechs had been under Austrian rule for centuries. Additionally, the Czechs and Slovaks share similar languages. The creation of Czechoslovakia was a way for the Czechs and the Slovaks to declare themselves independent from the Habsburg Empire. World War I ended in 1918 with the defeat of the Central Powers, which included Austria-Hungary. With the support of U.S. President Woodrow Wilson for the autonomy of the nations comprising Austria-Hungary, the Republic of Czechoslovakia was recognized internationally.

From the beginning of the new Czechoslovak nation there were problems. Even though the Czech lands and Slovakia had shared a similar pattern of historical events up until the ninth century, a thousand years under the control of separate nations had created different histories, in turn affecting religious, economic, political, and social traditions. By 1918 the Czech lands had been urbanized to a much greater extent due to the fact that Bohemia (the western region of the Czech lands) had been the most industrial area of the Habsburg Empire. In Slovakia the land was largely rural, with a majority of the people subsisting from agriculture. Additionally, Slovaks were not as educated as their counterparts nor had they much experience in self-governing. As a result of all of these factors, the Czechs took a greater role in the development of the Czechoslovak state. Slovaks began to feel discontent with the centralized government control, now based in Prague, and what was perceived by many as Czech economic and political domination.

Between the two World Wars, Czechoslovakia was made up of the following regions: Bohemia and Moravia combined to form the Czech lands in the west, and Slovakia (with Subcarpathian Rus until 1939) comprised the land in the east. Together the Czechs and Slovaks made up two-thirds of the ethnic population of the First Czechoslovak Republic (1918-1938).

Courtesy of Wikipedia

One of the larger minority groups was the Germans who had settled in Bohemia and Moravia along the border with Germany, Austria, and Silesia, part of it being called "Sudetenland." When Hitler came to power in Germany, the significance of this area increased because of his interest in the "Germans" who resided there and also because of the value of Bohemia and Silesia as important industrialized areas. Hitler exploited conflicts between the German minority and the Slavic majority in Czechoslovakia and used this conflict as his pretext to step in and begin his occupation of Central Europe.

The Munich Agreement was signed in 1938 by Hitler and the leaders of Britain, France, and Italy. Its purpose was to avert Hitler's aggression over Europe by ceding the German-speaking areas of Bohemia and Moravia to Germany. Czechoslovakia was not invited to join the discussion and their opinions were not sought. With the threat of war, the German-speaking areas went to Germany, as well as one-third of Slovak territory ceded to Hungary and a small area to Poland. A greatly weakened Czechoslovakia was ready to fall into German hands, as Hitler had planned from the outset.

To precipitate this, Hitler maneuvered the Slovak leader Jozef Tiso into breaking with Czechoslovakia by declaring Slovak independence. What would have been the alternative if Slovakia had not stepped away from Czechoslovakia and declared its independence? Hitler would have allowed the remaining Slovak territory to be partitioned between Hungary and Poland. In the end there was no choice.

The Slovak Parliament declared the establishment of the First Slovak Republic on March 14, 1939, and the next day the Germans invaded Bohemia and Moravia. Until the end of World War II in 1945, Slovakia was conceptually independent, but in reality it was subject to Nazi Germany. On the one hand, there were positive effects, including an economic boom that occurred due to war time production, and the fact that Slovakia avoided battles on its soil for most of the war. On the other hand, independence was largely an illusion based on Nazi cooperation.

In 1944, Slovak troops (organized mostly by Slovaks exiled abroad) rose up against the Nazis and the sympathizing Slovak government. The revolt, which lasted two months, is known as the Slovak National Uprising, and though it was put down by the German forces, this act of resistance has since assumed historical significance. This was the period when Slovakia changed sides to support the Allies. The Germans occupied Slovakia until the close of World War II when Soviet troops liberated Slovakia, Moravia, and most of Bohemia, supported by Czech and Slovak resistance forces.

NOTE

August 29 is a Slovak holiday, the anniversary of the National Uprising. May 8 is a holiday both in Slovakia and in many European countries. It is Victory in Europe day, the anniversary of the end of WWII.

Czechoslovakia was reinstated in April 1945 and regained territories that it lost under the Munich Agreement. The German population was expelled, mostly to Germany, and Hungary and Slovakia exchanged a number of citizens back into their ethnic countries. The Soviets occupied the Rusyn region—the eastern most area on the border with Ukraine called Subcarpathian Rus—and later officially annexed it. Being kindly disposed to the Soviet Army as well as being disappointed with the West and the Munich Agreement, the Czechoslovak government by the end of the war was ready to strengthen its Soviet alliance.

Communist representation in government increased by the elections in 1946 but not enough to claim victory. Though the communists did not have a majority in the government cabinet, they had managed to gain control over key ministries by February 1948, such as the Ministry of the Interior which included control of the state police. The government became increasingly dysfunctional when non-communist cabinet members demanded that the communists stop using their power to suppress non-communists. Many cabinet members resigned in protest and with the intention of forcing President Beneš to call for new general elections.

At first President Beneš refused to accept their resignations or to call for new elections. When the communists began arming a workers' militia, Beneš accepted new communist party candidates as replacements, perhaps to avoid intervention by the Soviets. This was the beginning of the communist era.

From 1948 to 1989 Czechoslovakia was almost entirely a model Soviet satellite state, subordinate to Soviet interests. The centrally planned economic model for Czechoslovakia was based on the Soviet model. Rapid development of heavy industry began, and the country became an important supplier of machinery and arms to other communist countries.

Submission to the Soviet Union came with a price. Large scale purges took place within the government to remove reformists from Czechoslovak leadership positions in the 1950s and again in the first half of the 1970s. This second round of purges occurred particularly as a result of the brief period of liberalization that took place in the earlier months of 1968 known as the "Prague Spring." The reforms of Slovak Alexander Dubček, then the Czechoslovak leader, were an attempt to put a "human face" on socialism in the form of liberalization and a call for greater democracy. The "Prague Spring" came to an end in August 1968 when 200,000 Warsaw Pact troops restored Soviet control once again.

As Czechoslovakia continued to evolve in the decades after World War II, many Slovaks wanted to see the development of two individual federal republics that would allow for increased Slovak autonomy rather than a single integrated, centralized system. It seemed that the Czechs viewed themselves as Czechoslovaks while Slovaks viewed themselves as Slovaks who were part of the Czechoslovak state.

Courtesy of Wikipedia

An issue that had not yet been resolved by 1950 was the imbalance between the Czechs and Slovaks in major areas such as industrialization and economics, politics, education, and health care. This imbalance became a priority for the post-1948 government, and there was vast improvement in these areas throughout the 1960s and 1970s. Despite this, the Czech-Slovak division remained. Particularly in the area of political development, the Czechs most often held the more senior positions and greater authority in government than Slovaks. This strengthened Slovak resolve to have more autonomy from the Czechs.

The overthrow of the communist government in Czechoslovakia happened with demonstrations that took place in Prague and Bratislava from November to December of 1989. It became known as the "Velvet Revolution" because the events that led to the end of communism were largely peaceful.

In 1992, Czechoslovakia was dissolved in what is now referred to as the "Velvet Divorce." In the end it wasn't the people who decided, but the politicians. Czech officials wanted a tighter federation while Slovak officials wanted a more confederal type of system. The issue became impossible to resolve and led to a peaceful division and the birth of two new nations on January 1, 1993.

An Independent Slovakia and the European Union

Though the birth of an independent nation is usually a reason for joy and celebration, the birth of Slovakia in January 1993 was tempered by a feeling of reluctance from those who didn't wish to see Czechoslovakia split. Furthermore, there were many who felt apprehension about the future of their tiny new nation. After a short while, however, there would be no changing the course of independent Slovakia.

As if establishing a new constitution and government wasn't enough of a change, consider the challenge of transitioning a centrally planned economy into a competitive market economy. At the beginning of this shift, many Slovaks thought that with the implementation of a market economy, living standards in Slovakia would catch up with the rest of Western Europe in about 10 years. After the ten year marker had come and gone, the situation was re-evaluated. A new forecast predicted that it would take Slovakia, as well as the rest of the former Eastern Block, 50 years before the standard of living could compare to the leading EU countries. According to the *Economic Survey of the Slovak Republic in 2007*, produced by the OECD, strong economic growth in recent years has narrowed the gap, but there is still a long way to go. GDP per capita in Slovakia is still approximately 51 percent of the average of the original 15 EU members.

Slovakia joined the European Union in 2004, and the planned date for adopting the euro as its currency is 2009. The country continues to integrate within Europe and grow politically and economically. For some, particularly older Slovaks and those who have difficulty being competitive in the changing labor market, change is happening too quickly and the price of reform is too high. For others, particularly younger Slovaks and those who live in and around the economically dynamic region of Bratislava, change is not happening fast enough.

A common trend for many young Slovaks is to search for and find work abroad, preferably in Western Europe. As more EU countries open their doors to labor from new EU member countries, Slovaks feel the pull to compete in the market economy by learning new skills outside of Slovakia and looking for better paying jobs than they can find at home. Is that a bad thing? Should there be concern for another new wave of emigration out of Slovakia? Not necessarily. For one reason, most have the intention of making money and returning to Slovakia. For another reason, Slovakia needs its people to gain experience abroad and bring that newly acquired know-how back home, to introduce new practices within the country.

REFERENCES

Csáky, Moritz and Elena Mannová. 1999 *Collective Identities in Central Europe in Modern Times*. Bratislava: Institute of History of the Slovak Academy of Sciences

Horák, Anna G. 1948. *Slovakia*. Prague: Sphynx Publishers Ltd.

INFOSTAT, Institute for Informatics and Statistics Bratislava, Slovak Republic, http://sodb.infostat.sk

Klein-Pejšová, Rebekah. 2007 *Among the Nationalities: Jewish Refugees, Jewish Nationality, and Czechoslovak Statebuilding*. PhD diss., Columbia University

Kováč, Dušan et al. 1998. *Kronika Slovenska 1 (Chronicle of Slovakia 1)*, 1st ed., Bratislava: Fortuna Print

Reimer, Thomas. 2005. *Carpathian German History*. http://www.geocities.com/ycrtmr/history.htm#History

Rothskirchen, Livia. 2000. *Holocaust Period-Slovakia* from Jewish History of the Czech Republic Web site: www.porges.net/JewishHistoryOfCzechRepub.html

History of Slovakia. 2007. Wikipedia: http://en.wikipedia.org/wiki/History_of_Slovakia

Hlavné námestie, or Main Square in Bratislava is in the foreground, with St. Martin's Cathedral and Bratislava castle in the background.

THE BASICS: THINGS YOU SHOULD KNOW

NATIONAL HOLIDAYS AND BUSINESS HOURS

Slovakia has 15 public holidays per year:

Table 3: National holidays

1 January	Day of the Slovak Republic
6 January	Epiphany
	Good Friday
	Easter Monday
1 May	Labor Day
8 May	Victory in Europe Day
5 July	The Feast of Saints Cyril and Methodius
29 August	Anniversary of the Slovak National Uprising
1 September	Day of the Slovak Constitution
15 September	Feast of the Virgin Mary, Patron of Slovakia
1 November	All Saints' Day
17 November	Fight for Freedom and Democracy Day
24 December	Christmas Eve
25 December	1st Christmas Day
26 December	2nd Christmas Day – St. Štefan's Day

Holidays are always observed on the days they fall. If a holiday falls on a Saturday or Sunday, the observance is not moved to the closest Friday or Monday, as is the custom in some other countries.

What are the possibilities of being able to go grocery shopping while there is a public holiday? In towns and cities the chances are very good. Unlike in some western European countries where the economy of an entire nation ceases to function on a holiday, many Slovak supermarkets, store chains, and even a few bank branches, usually located within large shopping malls, stay open. And just what do I mean when I refer to a town? I lived in a small town in western Slovakia with a population of approximately 15,000 people. In town there are two large supermarkets with an excellent variety of foods and products, and with extended store hours.

In the last few years supermarkets have sprung up nationwide, and the convenience they have brought is palpable. There are also small, privately-owned shops that sell groceries and have extended hours. These shops can be found in small towns and villages as well. The only days where store hours would not be extended are for the solemn observance of the Easter and Christmas holidays.

Business hours vary slightly, but most office hours begin at 8:00 or 9:00 am and finish at 5:00 or 6:00 pm. The working hours for shops depend on the type of business. Grocers, bakers, butchers, and other small shops open as early as 6:00 am. General stores like clothing or bookstores open from 9:00 am until 6:00 pm. In many smaller towns and villages, stores and public buildings such as banks and the post office are closed for lunch. These times vary between 12:00 pm and 1:30 pm for half an hour or an hour. On Saturdays, many of the smaller, privately owned and privately-run shops close at 12:00 pm for the day. You can expect these kinds of small shops to be closed on Sundays also. The large supermarkets or mall shops stay open on Saturdays and Sundays.

One major exception to regular business hours that can be very frustrating is with some government offices. For example, departments such as the Labor Office or the Office of the Foreign Police have hours such as Mondays from 8:00 am until 3:00 pm; Wednesdays, 8:00 am to 5:00 pm; and Fridays, 7:30 am until 12:00 pm (and don't forget the lunch break from 12:00 pm to 1:00 pm!); Tuesdays and Thursdays they are closed. Times are subject to change, so be sure to have someone help you call ahead to check on availability, or you could be making a trip for nothing.

CLIMATE

Slovakia has a continental climate with four distinct seasons. The winters are usually cold and wet, while the summers are warm. You can expect rain year-round, so keep that umbrella close at hand. In Bratislava the average annual rainfall is 26 inches (650mm) with the temperatures ranging from 27°F to 36°F in January (-3°C to 2°C) and from 61°F to 79°F in July (16°C to 26°C). Temperatures in the north of the country as well as in the mountains are much cooler.

When thinking about what kinds of clothing to bring, consider layering. For winter weather, the absolute necessities are a good heavy coat or thick jacket and a pair of sturdy winter shoes. Items like sweaters, scarves, and gloves are standard, of course, but if you are planning to make a move and are short on packing space, keep in mind that you can buy items like these in Slovakia without too much hassle.

The stores and shops have a pretty good selection and basically, whatever you have at home you can find in Slovakia. Sporting goods stores carry a range of high quality jackets and gear (remember, there are the Tatra Mountains for skiing enthusiasts), but you probably won't find the deals you would at home.

In the summer it can be pretty warm and sticky, particularly in the larger cities, so the lighter the better. During the day the humidity can sometimes make it feel ten degrees hotter than it really is. When the evening comes around, if you're unprepared, don't be surprised if a thunderstorm sneaks up from out of nowhere.

Enjoying the winter weather in the mountains

ARRIVING TO SLOVAKIA AND CROSSING BORDERS

When considering the best way to travel into Slovakia, you have a variety of means to choose from. If Slovakia is your final destination and you are planning to buy a plane ticket, you have the possibility of looking into flights for either Bratislava or Vienna as your point of arrival. If your final destination is Eastern Slovakia, it might be better to fly to Košice. Czech Airlines has direct flights from Prague to

Košice, Žilina, Poprad, and Sliač, as well as to Bratislava. Austrian Airlines also has direct flights from Vienna to Košice.

The M. R. Štefánik, International Airport in Bratislava www.letiskobratislava.sk is a small airport, conveniently located only 15 minutes from the city center. There is a bus stop directly next to the terminal and, of course, taxi services available. Because of the airport's small size, it's easy to make your way through. The airport is rapidly expanding to accept new flights and carriers, which means that you might find a flight reservation that is less complicated and priced comparably as flights into Vienna.

M. R. Štefánik International Airport in Bratislava

For those who are not flying into Bratislava, flying into Vienna is a feasible alternative. Schwechat International Airport www.viennaairport.com is located just outside the city of Vienna to the east and is about 60 kilometers (37 miles) from Bratislava. Buses run more or less hourly from Schwechat to Bratislava, with the first bus leaving at 8:25 am and the last one leaving at 11:25 pm. The transit time is about an hour and 10 minutes. Tickets can be purchased from the automated machine located just outside the doors of the departure area, and the cost is somewhere between €8 or €9 ($11 to $12 USD) one way. You can purchase a round-trip ticket for convenience if you will be returning to the airport. If you buy a round-trip ticket, the return trip is left open-ended and valid for three months. Just remember that when you want to return, you have to make a reservation for the time your bus will depart from the Mlynské Nivy bus station in Bratislava. You can make the reservation at the ticket office inside the bus station. The departure schedule from Schwechat to Bratislava is as follows:

Table 4: Bus schedule, Vienna Schwechat > Bratislava

8:25	9:25	10:35	11:25	12:25	13:25	14:25	
15:25	16:25	17:25	18:25	19:35	20:25	21:55	23:25

If you have a late flight into Schwechat and don't plan to travel to Bratislava until morning, be aware that the cost of the hotels near the airport is very expensive, and if you want to shop around for cheaper rates, the drive to Vienna is approximately 30 minutes. Another option besides taking a bus to Bratislava, is paying about €60 ($81.60 USD) for a taxi. When looking for a taxicab company, consider Slovak taxis over Austrian taxis; the price will be much cheaper. Arranging a taxi might even be something done in advance. There is a taxi service called 01 Taxi Schwechat SK, www.01taxi.szm.sk that charges 1500 Skk (€44.20, or $60.50 USD), which even has a telephone number for English speakers. Arranging this kind of service might be preferable to prevent being overcharged.

You might be tempted to look into Budapest, Hungary as another point of arrival on your way to Bratislava, but unless you have a purpose for arriving in Budapest first, it probably isn't such a good idea. The travel time from

Budapest to Bratislava is approximately two and a half to three hours by either bus or train, and with heavy luggage, it would be more of a hassle than its worth.

Since the accession of Slovakia into the EU in May 2004, the process of crossing borders has become a lot easier. EU citizens don't need to carry passports to travel between the EU nations that still maintain border crossings, such as the latest EU accession members of the Czech Republic, Slovakia, Poland, Hungary, etc. Instead, EU citizens can make do with national identification cards.

Additionally, Slovakia is a member of the Schengen Agreement. The Schengen Agreement is an agreement among European countries that allow for common policy on the temporary entry of people, and for the harmonization of border controls. Slovakia signed the Schengen agreement when joining the EU in 2004 but has not yet implemented the agreement. Implementation is scheduled for late 2007 once all of the preparedness requirements are met. Until then, border crossing procedures will be maintained. All nationals from non-EU nations must carry a passport, which will be checked and possibly stamped while crossing into Slovakia. Also, the visa policy has been harmonized, which means if you need a visa for the Schengen Zone, the visa will cover your entrance into Slovakia.

If you are an American, Canadian, or Australian, you don't need a visa to cross into Slovakia for a short-term stay—that is, fewer than 90 days. Citizens from these countries have an automatic 90-day traveler's visa that doesn't require any paperwork or fees. Just make sure that your passport doesn't expire within six months of the last day you plan to be in the country.

For a stay in Slovakia lasting longer than 90 days, additional documents will be required for legal employment, study, or extended stay for reunion purposes, but are not needed on first arrival as proof of stay in Slovakia.

See chapter 4 on "The Law" for further information on visa preparation.

SEE MORE

It's a good idea to make a copy of your passport identification page and keep it somewhere else just in case your passport gets lost or stolen. Also, keep the contact information inside the passport up to date.

As a foreigner, you are required to have your passport with you at all times. It is your primary means of identification, so keep it safe.

ATTENTION

Since 2002, the law states that all foreign visitors entering the country are required to have medical insurance valid in the Slovak Republic, and at least 50 USD (or equivalent in another currency, travelers checks, or a credit card) per day of their stay in the Slovak republic. From my own personal experience of traveling between Austria and Slovakia for the last several years, I have never been asked to show proof of either of these requirements, nor have I ever known anyone who has. I have heard the Slovak news report that Slovak border agents have asked for these requirements from Croatian citizens to reciprocate for Croatian border agents asking the same of Slovak citizens.

TRANSPORTATION AND TRAVEL

The following pages contain descriptions of various forms of transportation to, from, and within Slovakia. Because the most common entry point into Slovakia is through Bratislava, descriptions of transportation in Bratislava are described in more detail.

INTERNATIONAL TRAVEL BY TRAIN

The most common type of travel in neighboring European countries to or from Slovakia is via rail. There are many train stations in Bratislava, but almost all international trains stop at *Bratislava Hlavná stanica* – Bratislava Main Train Station. There is also a second international train station in Bratislava called *Železničná stanica Bratislava-Petržalka* – Bratislava-Petržalka Train Station. The most efficient way to obtain information on train schedules and ticket prices is through the Internet. A good Web site is www.slovakrail.sk.

A train approaching at Bratislava Hlavná stanica

From *Bratislava Hlavná stanica*, railway routes converge from Austria, the Czech Republic, Poland, Hungary, and Ukraine. The following table outlines the major train routes, by direction, from Slovakia to its neighboring countries, through *Bratislava Hlavná stanica*:

Table 5: International train routes - *Bratislava Hlavná stanica*

Austria	direction Vienna via Marchegg	direction Vienna via Petržalka and Kittsee
	Bratislava Devínska Nová Ves Marchegg Vienna Sudbahnhof	Bratislava-Petržalka Kitsee Bruck a.d. Leitha Vienna Sudbahnhof
Czech Republic	direction Berlin - Dresden	direction Warsaw - Katowice
	Bratislava Kúty Břeclav Brno Prague Děčín	Bratislava Kúty Břeclav Otrokovice Ostrava
Poland	direction Krakow	direction Warsaw
	Bratislava Trnava Trenčín Žilina Čadca Krakow	Bratislava Kúty Břeclav Otrokovice Ostrava Warsaw
Hungary	direction Budapest via Nové Zámky	direction Budapest via Györ
	Bratislava Galanta Nové Zámky Štúrovo Szob Budapest	Bratislava Rajka Györ Budapest

Express trains are marked with an "R", which stands for *rýchlik* – fast train. These trains make fewer stops, while slower trains are marked with "Os", *osobný vlak* – or passenger train, which make many stops.

INTERNATIONAL TRAVEL BY PLANE

In the last few years, flights by low-cost carriers such as Sky Europe and Ryan Air have become another means of inter-continental travel. Airports in Bratislava and Košice are handling an increasing number of air travelers. Round-trip flights from Stansted, UK to Bratislava can be as cheap as £50. Bratislava in particular has seen an increase in tourism as more Europeans take advantage of low-cost airfare to visit the city for a week-end trip.

INTERNATIONAL TRAVEL BY BUS

In addition to trains and planes, there is a network of buses that travel to larger European cities. The main bus station that is the hub for international and national bus lines is *Autobusová stanica Mlynské Nivy* (it's enough to say *autobusová stanica* – bus station, and a Bratislavan will know what you are talking about). There is a direct link to the main bus station from the main train station via trolleybus #210. International bus lines are run by *Eurolines* and provide service to places as far away as Paris and London. Their Web site is www.eurolines.com. The tickets are purchased in advance at the *Eurolines* ticket window located inside the main bus station. It is slightly cheaper to travel via bus, but you might miss the comforts you can find on a train or plane. Also, train and air travel tends to be quicker, although this is not always the case, particularly for shorter distances. Another useful Web site for information on trains and buses traveling to or from Slovakia is www.cp.sk. The site is accessible in English as well as in Slovak. In addition to international travel information, it can provide you with schedules within Slovakia.

Bratislava is a great starting point from which to make trips out to other international cities. If you are living in Slovakia for a long period of time, you'll want to take advantage of your great location in Central Europe to visit neighboring countries. The most common places to visit for a short trip or a weekend getaway are Vienna, Prague, and Budapest. To avoid pricey ticket fees charged in other countries, be sure to buy a round-trip ticket, rather than just a one-way ticket, in Slovakia. Traveling abroad can be expensive, especially after you've gotten used to moderately priced Slovakia. Depending on your financial situation, and particularly if you are living off a Slovak wage, you might not be able to travel as much as you would like. However with good planning, reasonable goals, and simple common sense, almost anything is feasible.

DOMESTIC TRAVEL BY TRAIN

If you won't have access to a car and you plan on traveling to larger towns in Slovakia, taking a train may be your best option; larger towns have good rail connections between them. The network outside of larger destinations is limited, however, and in this case, bus travel is used more extensively.

As mentioned previously, the simplest way to get train schedule information is to look online. If, however, you are already at *Bratislava Hlavná stanica* without having gathered information beforehand, there is an information office up the few stairs off of the main entrance hall, on the right-hand side, down a small hallway. In my experience, the information officers speak English and have been very helpful. They can even print out a schedule for you.

If you are determined to figure out train schedules on your own, schedules of trains departing for the day are located on the pillars of the main hall. There are four tables of departure times, one for each of the following directions: East, North, Northwest, and West. The tables, however, are not titled 'East' or 'West.' They are called by the name of a town that lies in a given direction. For example, the table entitled *Smer Kúty* (*smer* – direction—and Kúty is a border town at the Czech-Slovak border) contains only departure times for trains that go to the Czech Republic and beyond, such as Berlin. Similarly, the table entitled *Smer Žilina* contains only departure times of trains that depart northbound through the town of Žilina. Therefore, a basic understanding of local geography is necessary to figure out which table to look at. For example, approximately ten trains go to Košice each day, but you won't find them on the 'northwest' or 'west' tables. You need to be looking at the 'north' or 'east' tables.

Schedules of daily departure times at the main train station in Bratislava

At all train stations in general, your train can depart from a different platform than what the table of departures says, due to last minute changes. Tables of departures are usually prepared for one year and they cannot reflect all temporary changes.

REMINDER Always check the electronic tables of departures that is in the main hall and usually on each platform. They show the most recent and actual information.

Train tickets are purchased from the ticket desk. If you are buying an international ticket, look for the *KVC/ Komplexné vybavenie cestujúcich* – complex customer services—ticket desk. Domestic tickets can be bought at any ticket desk. For train travel within Slovakia, the amount you pay for your train ticket depends on the distance you travel (number of kilometers) and on your age (children below 15 and seniors above 60 pay less). University students are also eligible for a discounted ticket price if they can prove their student status.

Each ticket contains information not only about your departure and destination towns, but also about the route for which the ticket is valid and the corresponding number of kilometers. For example, if you are traveling from Bratislava to Košice, the major towns along the way will be listed on the ticket. Generally speaking, you can take any train between the two destinations specified on your ticket, but be sure that the train you board takes the route which is on your ticket and for which you paid. For example, there are approximately ten trains from Bratislava to Košice each day. If you buy a ticket that routes through Žilina and you board a train that routes through Zvolen, it will be necessary to pay the difference in price to the conductor.

Each ticket also contains information on the period for which travel is valid. Without a seat reservation, one-way tickets are usually valid for 1-2 days; round-trip tickets for domestic travel are valid for three days, for example from Bratislava to Košice and back. Round-trip tickets for international travel are valid for one month, for example from Bratislava to Prague and back. If, say, you buy a round-trip ticket from Bratislava to Košice that is valid for three days (from 24.02.2008 – 26.02.2008), departure from Bratislava can't be before midnight February 24, and your return back to Bratislava must occur by midnight February 26.

Tickets are sold one-way or round-trip. A more common name for "round-trip" is "return." A "return ticket" means a trip to another location and back. For domestic travel there is no discount on return tickets: you pay exactly twice as much as for a one-way ticket. For international travel, a return ticket is cheaper than the total cost of paying two one-way tickets.

When purchasing your ticket, you have the option of buying a *miestenka* – reservation. The cost of the *miestenka* is a fraction of the price of the ticket. Paying for a seat reservation is a wise choice, particularly if you are going a longer distance. Trains can be crowded between major cities, especially Fridays and Sundays when university students and commuting workers are either traveling home or returning for school or work.

Some specific trains such as the InterCity *Tatran* or InterCity *Kriváň* are *povinne miestenkové*, which means that you must have a seat reservation to board the train. In this case, the seat reservation will be automatically included in the price and your seat number will be printed on your ticket. In all other cases of train travel, a separate ticket is printed, detailing the seat reservation, train, car, and seat numbers.

Train tickets are typically packed with lots of information. If you are unfamiliar with the layout, deciphering a ticket can be a frustrating task. There are several different types of tickets; they all display the same information, more or less, just in slightly different formats.

The following is a sample domestic train ticket with a reservation:

Table 6: Reading a domestic train ticket

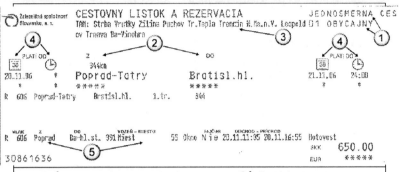

1 – *Jednosmerná cesta* – one-way ticket, *Obyčajný* – full fair
2 – Valid ticket use from Poprad-Tatry station to Bratislava hlavná stanica
3 – The list of towns/villages the train passes through along the journey
4 – Valid for 24 hours from 20.11.06 until 21.11.06
5 – Reservation: R = *rýchlik* – express train, number 606 from Poprad to Bratislava, car number 391, seat 55-window, no smoking, departure time 11:35am – arrival time 4:55pm

When looking for the correct train car to board, the train car number is typically a printed sign that is taped onto the train car door or close to the door. The sign also says the name of the train along with the names of the departure and destination cities. Once on board, markers displaying seat numbers and whether a seat is reserved or not are located outside the cabin if in a cabin car, or above the seats on the storage shelf in a train car with rows of seats.

If you buy a ticket without a reservation, you must find a seat on the train on a first-come-first-serve basis. This means you board the train, look for the marking that says if a seat is reserved or not, and if no one is there before you, you can take the seat.

Seats are marked reserved even if the seat is reserved only for a portion of a longer journey. For example, the train goes from Budapest to Prague, but the seat is reserved only from Breclav to Prague. Since you don't know from which point the seat is reserved, it is possible to take the seat if you don't have a reservation, but you will have to move once the person who has reserved the seat has boarded. To avoid this uncertainty, and to avoid the possibility of not finding a seat at all, buy a reservation along with your ticket.

NOTE

If you take a train without purchasing a ticket first, you may purchase a ticket from the conductor, cash only, but the price will be a bit higher.

For planned over-night travel, it is a good idea to purchase a reservation for a couchette or a bed. Beds are more comfortable and more expensive than couchettes: one second-class compartment with beds takes three people, a compartment with couchettes takes six people. The process of buying a couchette or a bed is exactly the same as for buying a seat reservation: specify the exact train you want to take and the exact date you want to travel, and the ticket teller at the purchase window will tell you if there is still availability. Your reservation will be printed as a separate ticket.

Domestic travel by Bus

The main bus station in Bratislava is *Autobusová stanica Mlynské Nivy*. Most bus lines are run by a Slovak national bus company called Slovak Lines, www.slovaklines.sk. The table of departure times is displayed on a large section of wall that you can't miss (in red and white) when you walk into the station hall.

NOTE

Hlavná stanica literally means "main station." However, if you ask for *hlavná stanica,* the person you are asking is likely going to give you directions to *Bratislava Hlavná stanica,* which is the main train station, not the main bus station.

To read the table at the Bratislava bus station, look for the name of your destination and you will see listed the times from the first bus in the morning until the last bus in the evening. Doesn't that sound simple? Of course there are going to be exceptions and that's what the small letters above the times indicate.

| *Rožňava* | 16 ‡ 0.25 | 26 ⓪ 1.00 | 21 ‡ 6.45 | 24 ‡ 9.45 | 16 ⱨ 10.00 | 14 ‡ 11.15 | 26 ⱨⱨ 11.20 | 16 ‡ 13.35 | 16 ‡ 14.00 | 26 ⱨⱨⱨ 14.00 | 1! |

| 21 ⱨⱨⱨ 17.00 | 16 ‡ 22.30 | 15 ‡ 23.35 |

| *Ružomberok* | 25 4.30 | 21 4.45 | 26 ⱨ 5.40 | 23 ‡ 6.30 | 21 ‡ 7.05 | 25 ‡ 8.20 | 22 ⱨ 10.20 | 24 ‡ 12.45 | 24 ⱨⱨ 13.40 | 24 ‡ 14.15 | 1 |

| 25 ⱨ 17.10 | 26 ‡ 18.00 |

| *Senec* | 21 ⱨⱨⱨ 4.15 | 21 ⱨⱨⱨ 4.15 | 25 4.30 | 11 ‡ 5.10 | 31 b 5.15 | 32 † 5.15 | 32 5.15 | 22 ⱨⱨⱨ 5.15 | 22 ⱨⱨⱨ 5.15 | 31 c 5.35 |

A portion of the bus schedule at the main bus station in Bratislava

It could be that you are traveling on a Sunday and not all buses operate on Sundays. On the left side of the entire schedule, there is a key with the meanings of various letters, which are also translated into English. Some are, for example, "weekdays only" or "Doesn't run on 25 Dec or 1 Jan." Once you have determined the departure time, you need to find out from which platform the bus is departing. The platform is indicated by the number above the time.

Boarding the bus for a regional destination

Most likely there will be a line of people who are patiently waiting on the platform for the bus to arrive. If you are unsure if you are on the right platform, ask someone. Even if you speak no Slovak, you can just ask the name of your destination, "Banská Bystrica?" and someone will likely affirm or negate. Once a bus has arrived at the platform, make sure you check the placard on the dashboard to be certain that you aren't boarding the wrong bus. Sometimes it turns out you are waiting for the bus that is coming after the one presently boarding passengers. For destinations farther than Banská Bystrica, a medium-sized town 200 kilometers east of Bratislava, you have the option of booking your ticket in advance at a ticket counter in the main hall. Otherwise, when boarding the bus for either a short or long destination, you will pay the driver, cash only, for the purchase of your ticket.

NOTE

Purchasing a ticket from the driver does not reserve you a seat. The driver sells as many tickets as people who can fill the bus. This means seats and standing room.

When boarding, tell the bus driver your destination. It is enough to simply state the name, and he will tell you the amount and print a receipt. The receipt is useful if you don't understand the amount he tells you. If you have *batožina* – luggage—it will most likely be placed in the storage area under the bus and a small fee will be added to your ticket total. If you have large pieces of luggage and the doors to the storage area are closed, it's best if you notify the driver before you pay for your ticket.

NOTE

When traveling on a bus trip longer than two hours, the bus driver will announce a *prestávka* – break—at a stop along the way, usually for 10 or 15 minutes.

Separate from what you'd see at the main bus station in Bratislava, the following is a sample bus schedule that is posted at an actual bus stop for national bus services:

Table 7: Reading a regional bus schedule

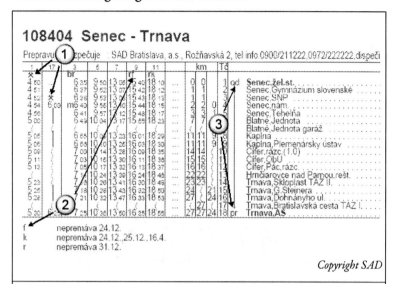

Copyright SAD

This type of schedule can be difficult to understand if you don't know what to look for. The most important things to know are where you are and where you want to go.

1 - The symbol 𝕏 means that the listed times are for buses going on a *pracovný deň* – or working day.

2 - Letters above or close to listed times indicate exceptions or special notes about that time. In this example, the letters *r* and *f* mean that buses *nepremáva* – do not run—on certain holidays in the year.

3 - The letters *od* and *pr* mean *odchod* and *príchod* – departure and arrival. In this example, the schedule is read from the direction of top to bottom. For return information, a schedule may be displayed to read from bottom to top.

LOCAL AND INTERCITY TRANSPORTATION

When traveling within larger Slovak cities, such as Bratislava and Košice, and to some extent in smaller towns, it is necessary to buy a pre-paid ticket for riding the *autobus* – bus, *trollejbus* – trolley-bus (a bus that makes use of overhead electrical wires), and *električka* – tram.

A Bratislava trollejbus

In Bratislava, for example, you are required to punch your ticket upon boarding. Travel is not valid until you punch your ticket. The same ticket is good for all three modes of travel and is sold at either newspaper kiosks or from yellow/orange automated machines that are usually located close to a bus or tram *zastávka* – stop.

The automated machines accept coins only.

NOTE

68

In Bratislava, tickets are priced according to the amount of travel time you may need and are sold in denominations of 10 minutes, 30 minutes, and an hour. Tickets are transferable but only for the time period from when it was first validated. For visitors needing more than longer coverage, there is a 24–hour ticket, a 48–hour ticket, and a 72–hour ticket. For longer term solutions there is a one, three, six, and twelve month pass. A discounted ticket is also needed for pieces of luggage larger than 30cm x 40cm x 60cm. Tickets are checked regularly by officials who come on board and ask to see your punched ticket. The fine for not having one is 100 times the price for one 10–minute ticket.

The local public transportation system is different in each town. In Košice, for example, tickets are not priced according to the amount of travel time but according to zones. Within a given zone, you pay the same price regardless of the number of stops you travel, and one ticket is valid for one ride only. If you change buses, you have to punch another ticket. So, even if you take only one stop by a bus line in Zone 1 and then transfer to another bus line and take only one stop again (still in Zone 1), you will need to punch two full-price tickets for Zone 1 (one per ride)—even if the total amount of your travel time might be less than 5 minutes. In the case that you cross zone borders on a bus ride, you need to punch two tickets (one for each zone).

Here are some general rules that apply to local public transportation in all Slovak cities:

- You need to have a valid ticket.
- You can buy your ticket at kiosks or automated machines, coins only; or from the driver upon boarding (except in Bratislava), exact change only.
- The ticket is invalid unless you punch it immediately upon boarding.
- The price of your ticket might depend on any of the following: travel time, number of zones, your age (children and seniors travel at a discount rate), and time of travel ("night lines" can be more expensive).

Within smaller towns and for travel between villages, a bus ticket is purchased from the driver when boarding. Bus schedules are posted at the local bus station or at all individual bus stops.

The following is an example of a local bus schedule for the city of Bratislava:

Table 8: Reading a local bus schedule

autobus **87** www.iMHD.sk	① ➤ Odchody zo zastávky: ASTRONOMICKÁ ➤ Smer: PETRŽALKA - OVSIŠTE ② Platnosť: OD **23.12.2006**		
čas, pásmo, poznámka, zastávka	pondelok - piatok (školský rok)	pondelok - piatok (školské prázdniny) ③	víkend, sviatok
	hod. minúta	hod. minúta	hod. minúta
← Astronomická	04 30 50	04 30 50	30 50
1 1 Astronomická	05 05 20 35 50	05 05 20 35 50	05 14 44
2 1 Súhvezdná ④	06 02 14 26 38 46 54	06 02 14 26 38 50	06 14 44
4 2• Váhostav	07 02 14 26 38 56	07 02 14 26 38 50	07 14 44
5 2• Vrakuňa - záhrady	08 14 34 54	08 02 14 34 54	08 14 44
6 2 Majerská	09 14 34 54	09 14 34 54	09 14 44
7• Šípová	10 14 34 54	10 14 34 54	10 14 44
8 2 Šíravská	11 14 34 54	11 14 34 54	11 14 44
9 2 Estónska	12 14 34 54	12 14 34 54	12 14 44
10 2 Stavbárska	13 14 31 46	13 14 31 46	13 14 44
12 2 Toryská	14 01 14 26 38 50	14 01 14 26 38 50	14 14 44
13 2 Podzáhradná	15 02 14 26 38 50	15 02 14 26 38 50	15 14 44
15 2 Slovnaftská ⑤	16 02 14 26 38 50	16 02 14 26 38 50	16 14 44
17 2• Závodná	17 02 14 26 38 54	17 02 14 26 38 54	17 14 44
18 2• Vlčie hrdlo - zastávka	18 14 34 54	18 14 34 54	18 14 44
20 1 Vlčie hrdlo	19 14 34 54	19 14 34 54	19 14 44
22 1• Čierny les	20 14 34 54	20 14 34 54	20 14 44
23 1• Terminál	21 14 34 54 ⑥	21 14 34 54	21 14 44
23 1• Pálenisko	22 14 44	22 14 44	22 14 44
24 1• Lúčna	23	23	23 25v
26 1 Prístav			
27 1• Mlynárenská		Poznámky	
29 1 Most Apollo			
31 1 Ekonomická univerzita	• - Zastávka je na znamenie		
33 1 Ovsištské nám.	v - Ide len po zastávku Vlčie hrdlo		
34 1 Ovsište	Čas - Priemerná jazdná doba na uvedenú zastávku v minútach Dopravca: DPB, a.s., Olejkárska 1, 81452 Bratislava.		

Copyright MHD

1 - Gives the name of the departure stop and the final destination.
2 - Schedules are updated at least once a year. The "effective from" date tells you when the schedule was last updated.
3 - Look up times according to the time of year: *školský rok* – school year, *školské prázdniny* –school break, or *víkend, sviatok* – weekend, holiday.
4 - The amount of time is listed in minutes from the boarding station. For example, this schedule is written for boarding at *Astronomická*, until your final destination. This helps when you aren't sure what increment of time to purchase on your ticket.
5 - On this route there are two tariff zones. This information is important for those who purchase a pre-paid pass of a single zone.
6 - Some routes have stops the driver will make only if requested by the passenger. These stops are marked with a dot. To signal a bus driver to stop when you are on board, press a signalling button, located near the exits of the bus.

TAKING A TAXI

In Slovakia, taxis are reasonably priced but there are a few quirks to keep in mind. One of the first things to know is that many taxi drivers think nothing about charging a foreigner more than the normal fare, just because they can likely get away with it. In Bratislava, for example, there are more than 15 different taxi companies and some drivers who are not signed up with any company at all. Taxis that are registered with a company are generally cheaper and safer; therefore, it is important to choose a taxi that has a taxi company label on the side of the car, rather than an unmarked car with just a taxi light on the roof. There are hot spots where taxi drivers are able to take advantage of unknowing tourists, and in Bratislava those places are usually in the historical center, hotels, train station, bus station, or airport.

How do you avoid being overcharged?

- Option #1: Have someone call a taxi for you. Calling a taxi ahead of time to meet you at a certain location and drop you off somewhere else is even cheaper than hailing a cab directly from the street. This also saves you the trouble of fixing a price and communicating with the driver where you need to go.

- Option #2: Agree to a price beforehand. Of course this can be a moot point if you are new to Slovakia, don't speak the language, or know what the average costs are to various locations. But once you learn costs and phrases like *Koľko stojí cesta do* ____ – How much to get to ____, the process gets easier.

- Option #3: Choose a taxi with identifiable markings on the car. If you can't call ahead for a taxi and don't have the ability to negotiate a price, at least make sure that your chances of getting a fair price are better by choosing a legitimate taxi service.

All taxis are equipped with a meter that shows you the charge. If you don't see a meter, it's an unlicensed taxi. When you get to your destination and are ready to pay, always round the total up to the next tenth, for example, 223 Skk becomes 230 Skk. Rounding up is the very least that is expected from the passenger. It is up to you whether you want to give an additional tip, though you might consider it, especially if the driver has helped you with luggage or is otherwise helpful or accommodating.

NOTE

You will not be offered a receipt automatically. Ask for a receipt if you need one.

CURRENCY AND MONEY MATTERS

The Slovak currency is the *koruna* – crown, with 100 *halierov* – haliers, making up one crown. The symbol for the crown is SK or SKK. The bill denominations come in 20s, 50s, 100s, 200s, 500s, 1,000s, and 5,000s. They are brightly colored and sized differently, making them easy to distinguish from one another. The coins come in denominations of 10, 5, 2, and 1 crown(s), with haliers coined only in a 50, half a crown. Cash is the most common method of payment, though use of ATMs or debit cards is also quite popular. Credit cards are not used as often and the personal check is nonexistent.

NOTE

Cashing a personal foreign check in Slovakia is possible but extremely complicated. Not only is the processing time lengthy, but the Slovak bank processing the check will charge a high fee.

Slovakia is part of the EU but isn't adopting the euro currency until at least 2009. In Bratislava, some of the larger department stores and large grocery chains accepts euros as a form of payment and give you crowns if there should be any change from your transaction. It's a good bet that as Slovakia becomes more integrated into the EU, more shops and stores will be capable of accepting euros. If you are considering using euros instead of Slovak crowns, just be sure to ask what the exchange rate is within each store and if there is a charge for paying in euros. There is the potential for some advantage taking, so shoppers, be aware!

When exchanging money, many places in very convenient locations would be happy to help you. Your best bet however, is at a bank. Though exchange rates are basically stable from one location to the next, the fees are not. Tatra Banka in particular is a wise choice when exchanging because there are many bank branches throughout Slovakia and they don't charge any fee at all. The Slovak crown is considered to be a 'soft currency' rather than the dollar and the euro, which are considered to be 'hard currency'. Because of this, make sure you use all of your crowns or exchange them back to another hard currency before you leave Slovakia permanently. Selling back your Slovak crowns once you return home could be difficult.

Before leaving on a trip many people wonder, "How much money should I bring?" The answer obviously depends on how long you are planning to stay, what your plans are, and if you are going to be working in Slovakia for some time, when you will be paid. In general, you don't need to bring a large amount of cash with you. Traveler's checks are accepted at banks and exchange offices with the exchange rate charge being at least one percent of the check's value. Also, there are many ATM machines throughout the country with the Cirrus® and Plus® Networks mark of acceptance for Visa® and Mastercard®, enabling you to withdraw from your bank account at home. You shouldn't be surprised, however, if there is an additional charge for international transactions.

While in Slovakia you may find yourself in need of paying a bill. In a billing statement of a cable bill for example, a *poštový peňažný poukaz* – or post office money order—is included. On this small piece of paper is listed the amount due, the bank account number and bank code of the company, and a reference number. To pay a bill, do one of the following:

- Go to a post office and pay it at the counter labeled *Úhrady* – payments.

- Go to your bank, fill out a *príkaz na úhradu* – payment order form—using the information from the money order. The money will be transferred from your account.

- Have the bill payment automatically deducted from your bank account. This process needs to be set up once in advance.

- Pay the bill through an internet banking transfer.

Internet banking can be activated with your account so that you can pay bills and make transactions without having to go to the bank in person.

SHOPPING

So, now you have your money and you're ready to do some shopping. When you walk in a store, particularly a smaller shop, you'll probably find a stack of baskets for customer use. Not only are these for your convenience, you should take one before you begin your shopping. The purpose of distributing the baskets is mainly for shop-keepers to regulate the maximum number of shoppers in a store at any given time. It's also possible that if the store is full and there are no baskets left, you will have to politely wait your turn until someone else finishes shopping and hands you the basket. You would possibly see this only in smaller food markets.

The price marked on an item often includes the tax, so there won't be anything else added at the register. Tax on items is called *daň z pridanej hodnoty* (DPH) – Value Added Tax (VAT). If a price does not include the tax in the marked price, you will see a sticker below it that reads, *Cena bez DPH* – Price marked without tax. VAT is 19 percent on all consumer products including food. A lower VAT is charged on medications and health-related products.

When you get to the cashier at a grocery store, you might be a little taken aback by the seemingly unfriendly attitude, or for being ignored all together. Certainly, many Slovak sales people won't win awards for western style customer service, but if you know what to expect it won't bother you so much.

Large supermarkets often provide plastic bags for bagging your groceries, though you will have to bag yourself. Small grocery stores sell large plastic bags with handles if you can't carry your purchases in hand and haven't brought a bag with you.

Busy weekend grocery shopping

In shops, when you are ready to make your purchase, a clerk may ask you, *Všetko bude?* – Will this be all? The answer may vary, of course, but often it is, *Áno, ďakujem* – Yes, thank you. Another good phrase to know when you are browsing in a shop and a shop assistant asks if you are looking for something is *Len pozerám, ďakujem* – Just looking around, thank you.

Return policies vary from store to store, but your chances of returning something successfully are slightly better than average if the item you are returning is still unused and tagged, and you have the store receipt. You'll probably never get your money back, but you might be able to exchange the item for something else if you have a legitimate complaint. And one more note: prices on items are generally fixed with no room for bargaining.

In the last several years, shopping centers have been built at a rapid rate in Bratislava. The city can now boast of five large shopping centers that sell everything such as home electronics, books, clothing, furniture, and of course, groceries:

- *Polus City Center*, www.poluscitycenter.sk, has a large supermarket and a movie theater complex among its attractions.
- *OC Danubia*, located in Petržalka, has a large supermarket.
- *Avion*, located close to the Bratislava airport, includes an *Ikea*.
- *Shopping Palace Zlaté Piesky*, www.shoppingpalace.sk/en, is the largest shopping mall in Slovakia.
- *Aupark*, www.aupark.sk, located in Petržalka close to the *Nový Most* - New Bridge, has a fitness center and movie complex.

If you can't find what you are looking for in Slovakia, it is easy to cross the border into Austria and do some shopping in Vienna. There are two shopping malls worth mentioning. The first is the *McArthur Glen Designer Outlet*, www.outletparndorf.at, located in the village of Parndorf, about 25 minutes outside of Bratislava across the Austrian border. The second is *Shopping City Süd*, www.scs.at, which is a huge shopping center located in the south of Vienna. The best clothing stores for different styles and reasonable prices are *C&A* and *H&M*, which are comparable to major department stores such as *Macy's* in America or *Marks & Spencer* in Great Britain.

Here is a list of some of the more popular department stores and chain stores:

Table 9: Chain stores

Tesco	A British department store and supermarket chain. Comparable to K-Mart or Wal-Mart in the United States, these stores carry a wide variety of goods and groceries at reasonable prices.
Billa, Kaufland	Major European supermarket chains with a wide selection of staple foods, international food products, and non-food items as well.
Coop-Jednota	A Slovak supermarket chain with the greatest number of locations throughout Slovakia, and with a good selection.
Lidl	A chain of discount stores with food and non-food items.
Metro	A chain that sells discount wholesale foods and products. Membership is required.
Baumax	A large chain store that sells hardware, home, and garden items.
Ikea	A large chain store that sells furniture and home accessories.
DM	A drugstore chain with an excellent range of goods, from hair care products to baby food.
Bat'a	A chain of quality shoe stores located through Slovakia and the Czech Republic.

SERVICES

Slovakia offers most of the same services that you are likely familiar with. Some of these include:

Table 10: Services

čistiareň – dry cleaner	*notár* – notary
opravovňa obuvy – shoe repair	*videopožičovňa* – video/ DVD rentals
kaderníctvo – hairdresser	*fotograf* – photography and processing
holičstvo – barber	*automechanik (autoservis)* – car repair
krajčír – tailor	*autoumyváreň* – car wash

Be aware that there are no laundromats. There are, however, private laundry services available in larger towns that wash clothing for their clients.

PRINT MEDIA IN ENGLISH

While you are in Slovakia you'll most likely want to keep in touch with current events and news at home. The simplest way to do this is by accessing your favorite sites through the Internet. If this is not an option for you, newspapers and magazines are a good alternative. In Bratislava and the larger cities throughout Slovakia, it's possible to buy the widely known international newspapers such as *The Herald Tribune, The Guardian, The Wall Street Journal Europe, USA Today,* or sometimes even *The New York Times,* or *The Washington Post.* Unfortunately, these newspapers are rather expensive.

In addition to international newspapers there is an English language newspaper that is produced within Slovakia called *The Slovak Spectator,* www.slovakspectator.sk. The newspaper is printed weekly and features the top stories as well as business and economic news, cultural profiles, and travel information. The Web site is updated daily through the workweek with the latest headlines. Another source for Slovak news in English on the Internet is the *News Agency of the Slovak Republic* (TASR) newswire, www.tasr.sk.

In Bratislava, a great place for reading English language newspapers and magazines without having to purchase them is at the British Council library located in the historic center, www.britishcouncil.org/slovakia. Admission is free, although if you are interested in checking out items, you will need to pay for a year-long library membership. In addition to newspapers and magazines they have a good selection of books, tapes, and DVDs in English. Their resources for English language instruction are particularly good. There are also British Councils in Banská Bystrica and in Košice.

NUMBERS AND CONVERSION EQUIVALENTS

Those of you who have traveled and shopped in other parts of the world where the systems of measurements and units are different know that you sometimes have a double challenge: asking for what you want in the local language and knowing how much to ask for. Converting the different kinds of measurements can take some getting used to, but obviously this gets easier with time and practice. Slovakia utilizes the metric system, the same as other European countries. The following are the most common points for numbering:

- The system for writing the date is *day, month,* and *year.* In Slovak, a date can be written as 26. máj 2004 or 26. 5. 2004; and occasionally you might see a date written with a Roman numeral for the month: 26. V. 2004.

- Large numbers require a space between the thousands, for example 14 326 664; or a period rather than a comma to separate the thousands, for example, 14.326.664. The comma is used instead of the period to mark a decimal, for example, 19,50%.

- Slovakia utilizes Daylight Savings Time along with the rest of Europe. The "summer-time period" of Daylight Savings Time in the EU begins on the last Sunday in March and ends on the last Sunday in October. Slovakia is located in the CET (Central European Time) 1 time zone. It is one hour ahead (+1) of London, +6 of New York, +9 of Los Angeles, −2 of Moscow, and −10 of Sydney. The twenty-four hour clock or "military-time" is used quite often, both in spoken communication as well as written.

- The standard electric current is 230 volts/ 50 Hz. If you are planning to bring a laptop computer that functions on a lower voltage, it shouldn't be a problem to use in Slovakia. Most modern laptops can automatically sense a change in voltage and adapt. You only need a plug adapter that attaches to the prongs to plug into the socket particular to Continental Europe. Check your laptop AC adapter for the information on input. If it reads *input: 100-240V,* then you're fine. Check your nearest retail department store or the Internet for a set of plug adapters. For any other electrical appliances or devices that need an adapter to work outside of your country, the best advice is not to bring them at all. It's simply too much bother to deal with power converters and to find additional plug adapters.

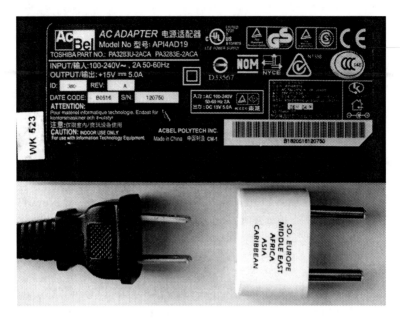

This North American power cord from a laptop computer can plug directly into an adapter without an additional converter because the input voltage of the power supply states 100-240V.

Depending on your knowledge and experience, the measurements you may or may not have to practice converting are the following:

- Temperature: Fahrenheit to Celsius

- Linear measurements: inches, feet, and miles to centimeters, meters, and kilometers

- Weight: pounds to kilograms

See Appendix D for a pocket list of conversions.

SEE MORE

VISITING A PUBLIC TOILET

Though the experience of visiting a restroom at a public location, such as at a train or bus station, isn't likely to present itself as an odd experience (flushing toilets are the norm in Slovakia as in most other European countries), the one thing you should know in advance is that you are likely to have to pay. Often there is a *hajzelbaba* – a slang term (and not to be used as a form of address) for a female bathroom attendant, who collects a fee, usually from two to five crowns. Toilet paper is usually distributed at the time of paying rather than in dispensers in the individual stalls. Still, it's good to be prepared with a packet of tissues.

HEALTH ISSUES

When you are going to be traveling and away from a health care system that you are familiar with, it makes sense to be in the best physical condition possible. Before coming to Slovakia, it's a good idea to be caught up on your general immunizations. A person should have a tetanus shot once every 10 years. If it's been more than ten years or you have never had a tetanus shot, ask your doctor about getting one. Vaccinations for Hepatitis A and B are purely precautionary and not mandated by the U.S. State Department for Americans when traveling to Europe. If you are applying for a long-stay visa, you will need a letter from your doctor stating that you have a clean bill of health. So while you are taking the time to see the doctor, why not make some appointments to have a few boosters?

If you have both work and residency permits in Slovakia and your employer regularly deducts taxes from your pay, you are entitled to health insurance. If you are without health insurance and you need to see a doctor, there are some private medical centers that offer general health care services, often for foreigners, and have staff who speak some English. You will be expected to pay by cash, or credit or debit card at your visit and, of course, prices are much higher at these private medical centers than state-run facilities that cater to patients with health care insurance. You can also expect that the quality of service will be higher. Most of theses medical centers are located in Bratislava. These are the addresses and phone numbers of a few:

Table 11: Private medical centers

Medifera Štúrova 12 811 01 Bratislava +421 (0)2 5720-0911 www.medifera.sk	Oralis (Dental care) NsP sv. Cyrila a Metoda Antolská 11 851 07 Bratislava tel: +421 (0)2 6381 0212 hotline: +421 (0)903 431 920 www.oralis.sk
Medius Daxnerovo námestie 3 821 08 Bratislava +421 (0)2 5596 9124	MUDr. Alexander Schill, (Dental Care) Baštová 7 811 03 Bratislava tel.: +421 (0)2 5464 7417 www.schill.sk
Top-Med, a.s. Cesta mládeže 1 831 33 Bratislava +421 (0)2 5465 1247 www.topmed.sk	Eurodent Medima, s.r.o (Dental care) Priehradka 20 036 01 Martin +421 (0)43 422 2447 www.medima.sk

If you need more specific information about the kinds of private medical care offered in the Bratislava area, a good source is the book *Easy Bratislava,* which provides a comprehensive list of doctors who speak English and their areas of specialization. The resources section on page 173 contains more information about this book.

For students traveling to Slovakia to study, getting a basic health insurance plan prior to arriving in Slovakia is recommended.

Supplemental insurance for foreigners is offered by Vzájomná životná poisťovňa, an insurance company. They can be contacted at:

Vzájomná životná poisťovňa
Špitálska 35
811 01 Bratislava
Tel./Fax: +421 (0)2 5296 8148
www.vszp.sk

If you see a doctor who prescribes you medication, you will need to go to the *lekáreň* – pharmacy/chemist—to have the prescription filled. Pharmacies also sell over-the-counter drugs as well, but for a wider selection of some products you might want to check out a *drogéria* – drug store/chemist. The most well-known drug store chain is called DM, which carries everything from toothbrushes to baby food. Although over-the-counter drugs are widely available in Slovakia, you will probably not find the same brands you use at home. If this concerns you, you should plan to make some room in your suitcase for commonly used drugstore items. Items like these might include pain medications, cold-flu medications, analgesic creams, band-aids, and of course refills of any medications you might be taking. You should also bring your optical prescription just in case you need to have new eyeglasses made.

You might be concerned that the quality of health care is not the same as the quality you would get in your home country. Though Slovakia and other former eastern-block countries are poorer than their western-European neighbors, the medical staff are trained professionals who provide satisfactory treatment. I personally have made plenty of trips to doctors' offices in Slovakia with the doctors being more than pleasant and patient both with me and the translator (most often a friend) who accompanied me. What you will likely notice is that facilities (not the staff) might be lacking and that policies are simply different. For example, in state-run facilities no one makes appointments to see a general physician; doctors see patients on a 'first come–first serve' basis, so patience is required in the waiting area. Often after doctors finish examining you, they process your paperwork themselves! They sit down at a typewriter or computer and type out your prognosis/prescription and stamp everything themselves rather than have an assistant do it. This just goes to show you that there are processes and policies different from what you might expect, not necessarily better or worse.

Waiting at the doctor's office

If you have special health concerns such as having particular allergies, or if you have special dietary needs, it may be difficult to meet your requirements. Though health foods and products with natural ingredients can be located in Slovakia, they are found sporadically throughout different grocery stores, and there are almost no health food stores to be found. The good news is that this is sure to change soon. "Bio" products are becoming more popular in Slovakia and are both vastly popular and commonplace in neighboring countries like Austria and the Czech Republic. It is only a matter of time before they are commonplace in Slovak cities as well.

THE LAW

VISAS AND EXTENDED STAY PERMITS

As mentioned in "Arriving to Slovakia and Crossing Borders" in chapter 3, a visa is not required for most entering into Slovakia for stays of fewer than 90 days.

SEE MORE

For a list of visa conditions of Slovakia with other countries, see the Web site of the Ministry of Foreign Affairs, www.mzv.sk, and navigate to Ministry > Travel Advice > Passports & Visas.

When planning to stay longer than 90 days and if you are not a citizen of the EU, you will need to apply for a temporary residence permit, also referred to as a long-term stay visa. Moving forward, I will refer to it as the temporary residence permit.

NOTE

Both the long-term stay visa and the temporary residence permit serve the same purpose. The difference between them has to do with where they are issued. A "visa" is issued at a foreign embassy in your home country while a "permit" is issued within the foreign country when you are already there.

The temporary residence permit is valid for only one year and must be renewed annually. Upon request, the temporary residence permit can be issued to an applicant after the applicant has arrived in Slovakia but the preparation of most of these documents needs to be completed in one's country of origin.

Citizens of the EU do not need a work permit or a temporary residence permit to be employed in Slovakia. All that is needed is for an employer to register them with the Slovak Labor Office, and with the Social Office. Those offices would then need to be informed when these workers have finished employment. It is also recommended, though not obligatory, that EU citizens register with the Slovak Foreign Police to submit an application for a residence permit, which is valid for five years.

Non-EU citizens must have a purpose for remaining in Slovakia in order to obtain a temporary residence permit. For most people applying for the temporary residence permit, the purpose is employment. Other purposes for applying are for business, study, or a family reunion.

Requirements for anyone applying for the temporary residence permit include a completed application that must be in Slovak, a preliminary job agreement from your future employer or notification of acceptance for study, a document confirming financial resources, documents confirming no criminal record in both Slovakia and your home country, and a document verifying accommodation such as a lease or rental agreement. Be sure to factor in the processing time of these documents when budgeting your time. You will need to have documents officially translated into Slovak and, with a rental agreement for example, notarized before submittal.

If your passport does not have at least one blank page for insertion of the permit document, you will need to have new pages inserted or get a new passport.

NOTE

U.S. embassies can insert extra pages into a passport if the passport is valid and all other pages have been exhausted. There is no charge for this.

When applying for the temporary residence permit, you must also provide proof of some kind of health insurance coverage that is valid in Slovakia. Even if you currently don't have health insurance but know you will have coverage once you begin legal employment in Slovakia, you must be insured for the gap of time between entering Slovakia and being employed in Slovakia. This might seem complicated but there are a couple of options. The simplest solution is to get international health insurance coverage for a set period of time. Another alternative is to look into getting Slovak insurance for foreigners.

SEE MORE

See the section "Health Issues" beginning on page 83 for more information on Slovak health insurance.

The document you need from the insurance company must have your personal data and the kind of coverage provided.

The work permit is provided by the Slovak Labor Office for "permission of employment" and is a requirement for the temporary residence permit if intending to work in Slovakia. It can take up to 30 days to process and is valid for up to one year. The work permit itself does not allow you to work in Slovakia but is validated only after completing the residence permit process. Also, work permits are issued for a specific employer and if you decide you want to take a job with a different employer, you won't be able to transfer the work permit easily.

ATTENTION

It can be tempting for some to consider the idea of working "black"—that is, without work permits or the long-term stay visa; but this is inadvisable. If you are caught, there are penalties to you as well as your employer. Thus, most employers consider the idea unfavorable.

If you plan to stay longer than just one year, it will be necessary to apply for an extension on your temporary residence permit. The application needs to be submitted along with the required documents at least 60 days before the expiration date of the temporary residence permit. Although the procedure is not as extensive as the initial permit application, it is still important to have everything complete and to apply for the extension on time. If your permit expires, you will have to start the process over from the very beginning. Applications can be obtained from the Foreign Police Office in Slovakia.

NOTE

Foreign Police officers generally do not speak English. Be sure to bring a translator to assist you in correctly processing your documents.

The fees for processing the application and some of the necessary documents are paid in the form of a special payment stamp called a *kolok*. These stamps – *kolky*—are different from postage stamps and are used specifically for the processing of government documents. These can be obtained at some kiosks where newspapers and magazines are sold or at the post office.

An example of kolky that have been processed as payment.

Does this sound daunting? Take it step by step and allow your future employer or school to help as much as possible. If they are experienced with the process of accepting foreigners, then they will know the correct steps to take. Don't be afraid to call the Slovak embassy in your country directly to ask questions or for clarification. The requirements (as well as the application fees) can change from one year to the next, so be sure to check online for the most up to date information and read everything very carefully.

For updated requirements and detailed information about visa requirements, the best place to look is an embassy Web site. For U.S. citizens it is www.slovakembassy-us.org; Canadian citizens, www.ottawa.mfa.sk; and for Australian citizens, www.slovakemb-aust.org.

SEE MORE   For more addresses and contacts for consulates and embassies of the Slovak Republic, go to the pages of the Slovak Ministry of Foreign Affairs at www.foreign.gov.sk or see www.mzv.sk.

DRIVING IN SLOVAKIA

The kinds of documents needed for driving in Slovakia vary according to citizenship. EU citizens may drive in Slovakia with their national license and do not require any additional documentation. All non-EU citizens are required to have an international driver's permit in addition to their national driver's license. This is also the case for any non-EU citizens who reside in Slovakia with a temporary residence permit.

So where do you get an international driver's permit? You might have to do a little searching, but mostly they are available from automobile associations that are authorized by the Department of State or Ministry of the Interior of your country. Look in the yellow pages under "automobile association" for a listing of locations and arrange to get the permit before you leave for Slovakia. The permit costs approximately $10 USD and is valid only for one year from the date stamped on the cover. If you do a search on the Internet, beware of claims offering to sell you an "international driver's license." There is no such thing as an international driver's license and advertisements trying to sell them are actually scams.

Though driving a car in Slovakia is like driving in most other continental European countries, there are a few traffic regulations that you should be aware of. Slovakia imposes a "road user fee" for certain public roads that applies to Slovaks and foreigners alike. For driving on the highways, it is necessary for your automobile to have a toll sticker that you place on the right side of the windshield. The toll sticker can be purchased at a border crossing, gas station, or post office and costs 1300Sk for a yearly sticker (*ročná*). A 15-day sticker and a monthly sticker are also available. Their prices change yearly.

Other important driving laws are as follows:

- Driving after drinking any amount of alcohol is prohibited. No degree of blood-alcohol content is tolerated.

- The use of mobile phones while driving is forbidden (though you may see drivers ignore this law).

- Seatbelts are compulsory for the driver and front passenger as well as for any rear passengers if the car is equipped with functioning rear seatbelts.

- Your car must be equipped with a reflector jacket, which you must wear while doing roadside repair.

- Headlights must be on at all times from October 15 until March 15. This will likely change to year– round soon.

- There is no turn on red—especially important for drivers from North America.

- Trams, trolleybuses, and buses have the right of way when turning right.

A roadway sign in Bratislava

If you are experienced with road signs and traffic laws on European roads and highways, then driving in Slovakia shouldn't be too different. Generally, signs are symbolic rather than textual. Moto Europa provides detailed information on international road signs at www.ideamerge.com/motoeuropa/roadsigns/.

Two octane grades of gasoline are usually available along with diesel. Regular unleaded gasoline or 'bezolovnatý' is usually marked with a green color.

Driving on a Slovak highway can be a challenge. Slovakia has few highways and most roads consist of a single lane in each direction. This often means that you must exercise caution when sharing the road with other cars, large transporting trucks, and sometimes even tractors. Passing or overtaking another vehicle is a skill you can expect to put to use if you drive in Slovakia.

Lastly, drivers in Slovakia have a reputation for being more aggressive than their western neighbors from Austria or Germany. It could have something to do with stiffer fines and penalties in western countries and the lack of fear of the consequences that many Slovak drivers have for breaking traffic rules in their own country. However, there is also a high death rate due to automobile-related accidents in Slovakia, including driving while intoxicated. If you are on a highway and see a small cross on the shoulder or something that looks vaguely similar to a tombstone, that's because it is. After someone has died on that particular stretch of road, loved ones erect a small marker in remembrance of their loss. You'd think that such a stark image would serve as a reminder to obey traffic laws and not drive aggressively. Unfortunately, it doesn't.

ATTENTION

If you are stopped by the police for violating a driving law, never offer a bribe to get out of a ticket. This is an offense punishable with jail time.

CRIME AND VIOLENCE

Compared to crime in many of the world's capitals, Bratislava seems quite tame, though crime does exist as in other larger cities and metropolitan areas. During the era of communism, serious street crime was virtually non-existent. But along with the numerous positive elements that came with the opening of the borders of "Eastern Europe," many of the negative aspects, such as drug abuse and organized crime, have taken root. Generally, the kinds of crimes that can be found in Bratislava and other larger cities in Slovakia range from pickpocketing and shoplifting to racially motivated hate crimes.

Pickpocketing is an issue at tourist destinations such as Bratislava's historic center, open air markets, exhibits, or fairs, and also on public transportation and in stations. A likely place for a wallet to be stolen is on a crowded bus or tram. A mistake that is often made is carrying something you can't keep your eye on. For women, avoid carrying purses that are worn backpack style when going somewhere that will be crowded, or if you do, keep your wallet or anything else valuable out of reach. Men typically carry their wallet in the back pocket of their pants. In a crowded place, this is an easy target, especially in summer when men usually wear only a t-shirt with no jacket or coat to cover their back pockets.

Another tip to prevent being picked by a pickpocket is to pay attention to your immediate surroundings. The good news is that up until now pickpockets have not been aggressive; in fact if you are a victim, you likely won't feel a thing. A good general rule to remember is that where there are crowds of people, there are very likely to be pickpockets.

Make a photocopy of your passport ID page in case your passport is lost or stolen.

REMINDER

The rise of racially motivated hate crimes is blamed on a variety of factors, including inadequate anti-discrimination legislation and enforcement. The victims of these crimes are most often Roma and foreigners, particularly non-whites. Additionally, skinhead-related acts of vandalism on Jewish cemeteries and synagogues persist, although not as frequently as in some other European countries. Also, though there are no laws against homosexuality, the homosexual lifestyle is not prominent within Slovak culture and there are few organizations or groups that are vocal on the issue of gay rights.

Another kind of crime that is common, particularly in Bratislava, is car theft. If you are driving a rental or a valuable car, the best advice is to park in guarded parking areas or at a hotel parking lot. Additionally, never leave anything of value in your car, and whenever possible don't leave anything in the car that could look as if it's covering something else, for example, a sweater or a blanket lying on the back seat.

You don't want to create any kind of perception that something of value is hidden beneath and inadvertently invite a curious thief.

Graffiti and tags under bridges are common.

Lastly, a crime that has developed more recently is that of hooliganism. With the introduction of cheaper air fare by low-cost airlines, the number of young, short-stay travelers has increased, particularly in Bratislava. Many come for stag parties or similar events, lured by cheap beer and comparably lower prices for accommodations. Though the increase in tourism is welcomed, the damage caused by unruly guests can bring more loss than profit. Municipal leaders in the Old Town of Bratislava are proactive in their attempts to curb hooliganism. These efforts include informing tourists of behavior that is considered hooliganism through leaflets placed at hotels and bars, and teaching some English to a special division of the police force to better handle situations before they can escalate.

CORRUPTION

The issue of corruption is something that is difficult to clearly define and even more difficult to measure. The Slovak government recognizes that corruption is a problem that needs continued vigilance on the path to complete integration within the EU. There is little doubt that corruption continues to remain an issue within Slovakia and all former communist countries.

Corruption is a problem ranging from paying a public-office clerk "on the side" to process paperwork faster, all the way up to the bidding of government tenders. Corruption is difficult to address because it affects various socio-economic groups and the blame is shared between the person who offers the bribe and the person who accepts it.

There is a generation of people, some of whom are not entirely ready to let the practice go and who, for example, would not think twice about offering a bribe to a doctor for better medical treatment. The process of changing the minds and attitudes of an entire society is complex and requires more time.

RELOCATING AND SETTLING IN

SLOVAKIA'S CAPITAL: BRATISLAVA

In many countries, the capital has a more developed infrastructure and greater economic opportunities for growth than its outside regions. Not only has this been the case with Bratislava, but in the last several years, a significant amount of foreign investment in Bratislava has further increased the gap between Slovakia's wealthier west and its poorer east. Though leaders in areas outside of Bratislava are attracting investors through the building of industrialized areas, greater opportunities in the Bratislava region continue to attract many investors as well as Slovaks from all parts of the country. They move to the city to study or work, and then remain permanently. The result is a capital city with a large mix of people from all regions of Slovakia. On weekends and particularly around major holidays, there is an exodus of people heading home or to their cottages in the country.

While Bratislava contributes much to its surrounding region and lies among other great cities of Central Europe, the city is markedly different from its nearest neighboring capitals of Vienna, Prague, and Budapest. For hundreds of years Vienna and Budapest were the capitals of their respectively vast Austrian and Hungarian empires. Prague shared the seat of the Holy Roman Empire with Vienna and also was the center of the most industrialized region in the Habsburg Empire. Their status as important historical, cultural, and financial centers continues to present day.

Courtesy of Miroslav Pokorný, Jr.

The newest addition to the Danube bank in Bratislava- Most Apollo

Though Bratislava was the capital of the Hungarian Empire from 1536 to 1784 while the Turks ruled Budapest— Bratislava was known by its German and Hungarian names of *Pressburg* and *Pozsony,* and also by its old Slovak name *Prešporok*—it never reached the level of influence or size as the other three capitals of the region. It was not the capital of its own (smaller, less powerful) country until briefly during the years of World War II and then from 1993. Unlike the three cities mentioned, Bratislava cannot be described in the same class historically or esthetically. This is not a criticism, but rather a reminder that Bratislava should be appreciated for its own qualities rather than simply compared to its other great neighboring capitals.

Bratislava has its own look and feel. Today, the *Staré Mesto* – Old Town—has many classic buildings from the baroque and art nouveau periods, but overall the city is liberally peppered with the odd mix of communist "socialist realism" architecture along with skyscrapers and a more modern style of architecture. The jumble of styles and sizes of buildings might leave you scratching your head, wondering if there was ever a master plan for the city. Or has development just happened, as it seems, in haphazard fashion.

Nový most and its recognizable UFO in the foreground of Petržalka

Consider for example, one of Bratislava's most visible landmarks, the *Nový most* – New Bridge (which many refer to as "the UFO bridge" because of its saucer-like top). This bridge was constructed in 1972 to connect the Petržalka area on the right side of the Danube bank with the Old Town on left side. The road that connects with the Old Town runs practically over the doorstep of St. Martin's Cathedral, arguably one of the most important historic landmarks in

Slovakia. Vehicles rumble by, just a few feet from the door of the cathedral where emperors and empresses were crowned, detracting from the building's stately atmosphere and shaking loose its fourteenth-century foundation. You wouldn't be the first to mumble to yourself, "Now, whose great idea was this anyway?"

St. Martin's Cathedral in Bratislava

With time comes change, however, and the city's skyline is changing rapidly. As more companies invest in property in Bratislava, areas such as the banks along the Danube are being developed with quality hotels, shopping areas, upscale apartments, and luxury office space. The city is constantly evolving and is home to 450,000 people who have a reputation for being open-minded and enthusiastic about creating opportunities.

HOW TO LOOK FOR ACCOMMODATION

When seeking accommodation in the Bratislava area, it's important to keep in mind a few things: first, despite the real-estate market boom and new construction projects in Bratislava, there is a shortage of housing. The renter's market is developed, and there are plenty of places found for rent, but the scarcity of housing is one of the major factors for pushing up prices well beyond the national average. Second, unless you speak Slovak, finding a suitable place without professional help or help from a local is challenging.

There are agencies specializing in providing short-or long-term apartment or hotel stays. Some good places to start are www.bratislavahotels.com or www.bratislava.info/ apartments/. Otherwise, to begin your search for housing, go to www.reality.sk, which is accessible in English, or www.reality.sme.sk which doesn't have an English version. For those who would like the assistance of a professional real-estate agent, there are many real-estate agencies in Bratislava. Several have English speaking employees and agents. It's a good idea to ask up front who pays the commission for finding a property: the landlord, the client, or both. Usually the fee that is charged is a month's rent averaged from a 12–month contract. For an extensive list of companies see the *Green Pages*, an English-language "yellow pages" provided by *The Slovak Spectator* at www.greenpages.sk/catg_real.html.

When reading descriptions of apartments for rent, you should know that "a two-room flat" means a kitchen, and "two rooms"—a living room and a bedroom. A separate dining room is rare. Words to describe the size of apartments are the following:

- *garsónka* – studio/bedsit
- *jednoizbový byt* – one-room apartment
- *dvojizbový byt* – two-room apartment
- *trojizbový byt* – three-room apartment

Sometimes you may also see ads for apartments like "2+1" or "2+kk." 2+1 means that the apartment has two rooms plus a separate room for the kitchen. 2+kk means that the apartment has two rooms with a "kk" in one of the rooms. The "kk" stands for the *kuchynský kút* – kitchen corner.

One thing that you won't find in a Slovak kitchen is a garbage disposal.

Some homes or apartments come already furnished. A furnished rental usually includes basic furniture such as a bed(s), a kitchen table and chairs, as well as basic appliances such as a refrigerator and freezer, a stove, and a washing machine. Nothing is guaranteed so be sure to ask for details.

It may be worth your while to obtain the services of a professional relocation company that can assist you with the many stages of settling in, including finding a house or apartment to rent, and assisting with enrolling children in the appropriate schools. One such company is called *Relocation,* www.relo.sk, and can help with everything from getting your long-term stay visa, to finding a housekeeper, or taking you on a supermarket shopping tour.

Where to live in Bratislava

The population of Bratislava is approximately 450,000 and is separated into five districts. The following are descriptions of particular areas in each district and details to consider when choosing a place to live:

I. *Staré Mesto* – (city center) The "Old Town" consists of the historical center and the area just below the castle. It's a very popular area with the expatriate community. Its positive points are that everything is within walking distance and it has good public transportation connections. Its shortcomings are the lack of public parking as well as the fact that it boasts of some of the most expensive property in Bratislava.

II. *Ružinov, Vrakuňa, and Podunajské Biskupice* – (east and southeast) Ružinov is another area popular with "expats" as it has good public transportation access and is rather an attractive neighborhood. Most of the possibilities for accommodation are in apartment blocks. The area within Ružinov that is more populated with residence housing is called Prievoz.

III. *Nové Mesto, Rača, and Vajnory* – (north and northeast) Nové Mesto is located just east of the Old Town and has the oldest apartment blocks in the city, some dating earlier than the 1920s. Access to public transportation in Nové Mesto is particularly good with many tram lines running through. Rača is located in the north-east of Bratislava at the beginning of the Small Carpathian Mountains and has some very beautiful surroundings of forest and sloping vineyards. It is not popular with foreigners mainly because of its poor access to the rest of the city. The main street that runs through Rača is called Račianska and can be a nightmare to drive, particularly during rush hours. Also in this third district are the areas of Koliba and Kramáre that are more popular with foreigners. Koliba is a hilly area close to Bratislava castle and to the town center with many expensive homes built up very compactly. Many roads in the area are winding and steep, making parking a challenge. Still, the view of the city below is great. Kramáre has both apartments and homes. A large hospital and emergency ward are located there.

IV. *Karlova Ves, Dúbravka, Lamač, Devín, Devínska Nová Ves, and the village Záhorská Bystrica* – (west) Karlova Ves is located in the northwest of Bratislava and is desirable to many "expats" looking for a house or an apartment, particularly for those who have children attending either of the two international schools that are located in the area. It is an attractive area with many tree-lined streets and a surrounding forest.

V. *Petržalka, Jarovce, Rusovce, and Čunovo* – (south) Petržalka lies on the right bank of the Danube River and is connected by a series of bridges with the rest of Bratislava. Though the area of Petržalka is not significant in size, it is extremely dense in population with one-third of Bratislava's population settled there. It is overwhelmingly a concrete jungle of panel blocks and is considered by many Slovaks and non-Slovaks to be an ugly environment. The positives are, however, the lower rent and relative closeness of grocery stores and businesses. Transportation to and from the other bank can be problematic though, as bridges are often blocked with traffic during rush hours and crossing can take some time.

THE RENTAL AGREEMENT

The basics of a rental agreement are covered by the Slovak civil code and include the following:

- Three months notice must be given for a landlord or a renter to break a lease early.
- A landlord can break the lease with a 7-day written notice if:
  - A renter sublets the apartment to a third party without the written approval of the landlord.
  - A renter breaches the contract.
  - A renter is late paying the lease or other costs involved for more than 7 days.
  - A renter causes significant damage to the landlord's property.
- A lease may or may not include payment for water and sewage, electricity, gas, cable TV, and phone. It may be the responsibility of the renter to pay these bills separately.
- A landlord is entitled to do construction, work, or other substantial changes on the property only after the renter has provided written approval.
- A renter must inform the landlord of any damage on the property. If the property is uninhabitable due to damage that is not caused by the renter, the contract can be terminated immediately.
- The landlord is obliged not to increase rent during the period stated on the lease. If both parties agree on lengthening the lease, the landlord can increase the rent based on the currency inflation rate or market prices.

A rental agreement does not need to be notarized to be legal. There are times, however, when you may need to have the rental agreement notarized, such as if the document is part of your visa application.

Household Appliances

Though standard household appliances such as a toaster, refrigerator, or microwave don't need much in the way of explanation, some differences in household appliances should be mentioned. Larger appliances, such as a washing machine or refrigerator, are typically smaller and more compact in Slovakia that what you see in North America. For example, one of the more interesting kitchen appliances is the stove-top oven unit with a dishwasher located in the second half, below the oven. This appliance isn't common in typical Slovak households but it is available.

A small appliance that you may or may not be familiar with is the electric kettle. Standard in the U.K. and pretty common all over Europe, the electric kettle is something like a plastic jug that you fill with water and set atop a fixed saucer with a central metal conduit. The electric kettle boils water much faster than conventional range kettles.

An electric kettle is standard in almost every Slovak's kitchen.

One thing that you will not find in a Slovak kitchen, or in many kitchens across Europe for that matter, is a garbage disposal in the sink. What do Europeans do when food goes bad and needs to be disposed of? Often it gets flushed down the toilet. I was shocked the first time I saw someone take a bowl of old potato salad to the toilet and flush it. It seemed unthinkable at first but soon I was following everyone else's example.

The dishwasher is becoming a standard fixture in Slovak kitchens, particularly for residents in larger towns and cities. On the other hand, a household appliance that is virtually non-existent in the Slovak market is the tumble-dryer. Almost all families make do with clotheslines outdoors, or when the weather is too cold, with a line "horse" that folds out for use. If you absolutely cannot live without tumble-dried clothes, driers are available on the Slovak market. The most interesting ones are the 2-in-1 combination washing machine and dryer that comes as a single unit. Again, nicely compact.

Heating in blocks of flats is regulated through a central location. Hot water access in houses is regulated either by a large water heater designated for use throughout the entire house, or regulated through smaller water heaters, located near fixtures that require them. You might see these water heaters close to the bath tub, shower, or in the basement, and small heater units above kitchen or bathroom sinks. The majority of these heaters self-regulate, and so it isn't necessary to fiddle with switches or worry that you will run out of hot water in a few minutes. Heater tanks do have a maximum capacity, so you might want to inquire if you'd be running out of hot water, say, if someone had taken a shower before you, for example.

TELEPHONE AND INTERNET

Emergency numbers in Slovakia are as follows:

Table 12: Emergency numbers

General Emergency	112
Police – *Polícia*	158
Fire – *Hasiči*	150
Ambulance – *Prvá pomoc*	155
Emergency road service	18124

An integrated emergency service has been implemented throughout many of the countries of the EU in which the number 112 is designated for emergency calls, much the same way 911 is used in the United States or 999 in Britain. In addition to the 112 emergency number, Slovakia operates the emergency numbers of 150, 155, and 158.

The country code for Slovakia is 421. The following is a fictitious telephone number in a national format for the area of Nitra: 037/7413 299. Using this number as an example, it is possible to see the different ways of calling, depending on where you are calling from.

Table 13: Telephoning and Slovak phone numbers

When outside of continental Europe and calling Slovakia	Each country has its own number to indicate that you are calling a number in a foreign country. For example, from North America you would dial 011 421 37 7413 299. See www.kropla.com/dialcode.htm for a more extensive list of numbers.
In Europe (Ireland, for example) and calling Slovakia	00421 37 7413 299

Table 13: Telephoning and Slovak phone numbers

In Slovakia (Bratislava, for example) and calling Nitra	037 7413 299 (notice that the area code is 37 and you need to dial the prefix of '0' when calling outside of your area code)
Calling from within Nitra	7413 299

Calling from Slovakia to any foreign country in the world requires 00, often written as "+", the country code and the national number. For North America, the country code is 1, for example 001 460 444-1234. Calling to another country in Europe, say Italy, requires 00, the country code (39) and the number.

Making calls and using the Internet can be less or more expensive depending on what time of the day you are calling. Rates increase during the *pracovný deň* – working day—which differs according to providers, but is approximately 7:00 am to 6:00 pm. Rates are also lower on weekends. Another option is calling through the Internet, for example, using Skype™. Calls between computers running Skype are free, and prices for calling from a computer through Skype to a landline are very low, especially for international calls.

Mobile phones and plans vary in price from expensive to fabulous offers that you can't pass up, and can be acquired quite easily. If you are going to be staying in Slovakia for longer than a few months, then a mobile with a number from a local provider is a must. For example, buying a prepaid package including a simple model mobile phone plus the telephone number is approximately 1,500 Skk to 3,000 Skk, approximately €42 to €85 or $60 to $120 USD. The three mobile phone operators are T-Mobile, www.t-mobile.sk; Orange, www.orange.sk; and Telefónica O2, www.sk.o2.com. T-Mobile and Orange provide an English version of their Web pages.

Another option is bringing a mobile phone from your country of origin for use with a Slovak SIM card purchased from a Slovak provider. Mobile phones in Europe function on GSM 900 and 1800 frequencies. If your phone doesn't receive both frequencies, your phone signal might be weak or may not function in some areas at all. Also, don't forget that you might need to buy a voltage-compatible charger.

Internet access is continuing its rapid growth throughout Slovakia and even in the smallest towns the chances are pretty good that you can find an Internet café to write a couple of e-mails home for a very low price. DSL, Wi-Fi, cable Internet, and cellular networks like GPRS, EDGE, and even 3G are becoming standard means of connecting to the Internet through Slovakia and are phasing out dial-up.

TELEVISION AND RADIO

Traditionally, public broadcast television stations in Slovakia have been state controlled. With the launch of private commercial television stations and paid subscriptions to cable and satellite TV, the market has become quite dynamic. Currently, three broadcast television stations are available through terrestrial broadcasting:

Table 14: Television and radio stations

Markíza – www.markiza.sk	STV – www.stv.sk (channels STV1 and STV2)
Joj – www.joj.sk	

The main cable and dish provider is UPC. More than 100 stations are available from their UPC Direct dish service. In addition to Slovak and Czech stations, there are numerous stations in English and German. Besides UPC, many cities and towns have their local cable provider.

Public Slovak radio is run at a national level with some of their more popular stations being *Rádio Slovensko* and *Rádio Devín*. Go to www.slovakradio.sk and click on Livestream in the menu for a list of stations.

Independently owned radio stations do coexist successfully alongside state radio. Some of the more popular, contemporary stations include the following:

FUN Rádio – www.funradio.sk	Rádio OKEY – www.okey.sk
Rádio Expres – www.expres.sk	N-Rádio – www.nradio.sk
Rádio_FM – www.radiofm.sk	Rádio Twist – www.twist.sk

As of January 2007, BBC World Service Radio has been discontinued in Slovakia. Slovak broadcasting law states that broadcasts can only be in a language that Slovaks understand, which means Slovak or Czech.

The government requires that residents who access television and radio provide a payment of a household tax. The tax is a relatively small fee used to finance public funding for programs that are to benefit society. If you have either a television or radio in your home, the fee will be included in your monthly rent.

The historic village of Vlkolínec

6

FOLK ART AND CULTURE

The folk tradition is alive and well throughout Slovakia. The country has a rich heritage that her people continue to enhance and pass on from generation to generation.

One of the best ways to experience Slovak folk tradition is to attend one of the many folk festivals that take place through the summer months. The biggest folk festivals are at Východná and Detva and they are widely attended. These festivals are a celebration of traditional dance and music as well as the traditional ways of life that are re-enacted around the village. Traditions include the many kinds of handcrafts, such as wood carving, ceramics and pottery, lace making, embroidery, the weaving of different kinds of metal wire, smithing, and brass work.

There are, of course, a variety of foods that can be sampled at such festivals, ranging from *turecký med* – Turkish honey—a kind of sweet meringue in a waffle cone, to *lokše* – a dough that is made with mashed potatoes, shaped like a flat pancake, cooked, and then rolled up with various salted fillings. Festivals are colorful, artistic, and vibrant events where you can see, first-hand, the folk traditions that are retained through art, crafts, food, music, and dance forms.

One summer I met a group of young Germans who said they had been coming to the Detva festival for the last several years. One man told me that the most amazing thing for him was to see the interest and participation of Slovak youth in folk culture. "In Germany," he said, "folk culture is for old people." This is definitely not the case at a folk festival where the range of ages is wide among participants. Quite often if you walk around the festival grounds at night after the performances are finished, you will see clusters of young people standing together playing instruments and singing folk songs.

A folk dance group from Zlaté Moravce

For a list of summer folk festivals throughout Slovakia, see "Seasonal Events" in chapter 7, on page 141.

SEE MORE

FOLK ENSEMBLES AND GROUPS

Slovak folk dance and music are art forms that have been passed down for hundreds of years. It is interesting that, although some people consider folk dance and music to be old-fashioned, they continue to play important roles in Slovak culture nonetheless. How so? A large part of the sustained presence of folk dance and music is due to the hundreds of folk groups and ensembles that originate in all regions of the country. Their members wear *kroj* when giving performances, which is a traditional folk costume decorated according to particular patterns of the region. Since there are variants of dance and music from the many regions and sub-regions across Slovakia, folk groups and ensembles create a kind of colorful map that distinguishes one area from another.

The difference between a folk group – *skupina,* and a folk ensemble – *súbor*, lies mostly in the degree of authenticity of their repertoire. *Skupiny* (plural form of *skupina*) are usually formed on the village level and consist of local people from a particular village or community. They carry on the Slovak folk art and traditions in their purest and most authentic form, passed down from generation to generation. *Súbory* (plural form of *súbor*), on the other hand, are based mostly in larger towns and cities, where ties to folk customs and traditions have, to a degree, weakened due to urban development and changing ways of life. When choreographers from *súbory* want to create a new dance, they would do field research and talk to people from *skupiny* in their region of interest, recording local melodies, dancing, and singing, and then they would create a dance out of all of it. Most *súbory* tend to concentrate on dances from regions in which they are based—i.e., ensembles based in eastern Slovakia would have dances mostly from eastern Slovakia, and so forth.

Some well-known Slovak ensembles include the following:

- *Ponitran*, *Zobor*, *Bezanka*, and *Kopaničiar* in western Slovakia
- *Marína*, *Podpoľanec*, *Váh*, *Stavbár* and *Magura* in central Slovakia
- *Železiar*, *Zemplín*, *Vranovčan* and *Šarišan* in eastern Slovakia

Almost all folk groups and ensembles in Slovakia are amateur, which does not mean that their performance is of a low quality, but rather that their members perform as their hobby and for the pleasure of it. There are, however, a few ensembles that are considered professional, meaning that they receive some sort of public funding (either through the Ministry of Culture or through regional governments) and that members who dance, sing, or play musical instruments perform as their job, or at least receive partial compensation for performances.

The most well-known professional ensembles in Slovakia are as follows:

- *Slovenský ľudový umelecký kolektív* (SĽUK) – The Slovak Folk Artistic Collective, www.sluk.sk
- *Umelecký súbor Lúčnica* – The Artistic Ensemble Lúčnica, www.lucnica.sk

Both SĽUK and Lúčnica are based in Bratislava and draw their repertoire from almost all Slovak folk regions such as *Zemplín*, *Šariš* (eastern Slovakia), *Liptov*, *Detva*, *Horehronie* (central Slovakia), or *Myjava* (western Slovakia). Most of their dances and music have been "artistically adjusted" for stage performance—in the Slovak language this is called *štylizované*—so that they look and sound better on the stage. So, while the music arrangement and choreography of their dances are beautiful to watch and listen to, in my opinion, they can sometimes lose the character of the regions they are supposed to represent.

For dances with a more regional and authentic feel, watch performances by regional ensembles listed earlier. To see Slovak folk art in its purest and most authentic form, watch performances by folk groups from particular villages. A general rule when it comes to Slovak folk dance and music is that the more local you go, the more authentic you get.

The best venues to see performances by various groups and ensembles are at folk festivals such as those in Myjava, Detva, and Východná in June and July each year, and the several other festivals that take place through the summer.

HOLIDAY TRADITIONS

Slovak holiday traditions have a great deal of history and symbolism. Depending on what region of Slovakia you are in, customs will vary. Here are a few of the more general traditions that are practiced across the country:

Veľká noc – **Easter:** The Easter season spans 40 days beginning with Ash Wednesday and building up to the holiest days in the year: the death and resurrection of Jesus Christ. The most significant days range from the Friday before Easter Sunday (Good Friday) to the Monday following Easter Sunday (Easter Monday). *Veľký piatok* – Good Friday is a work holiday, as well as *Veľkonočný pondelok* – Easter Monday.

The Easter season has special religious traditions such as the fasting of meat on Fridays (though some people, particularly in the rural areas, fast from meat on Fridays all year long). Furthermore, for Catholics, no weddings are scheduled during this time. Many of the rituals surrounding the holiday have pagan roots based around the changing seasons.

An example of a tradition with pagan roots occurs on Easter Monday. It is customary for the women to stay at home while the men, usually dressed in nicer clothing or even sometimes in traditional costumes, go from the residence of one relative to the next, bringing greetings and intending to *oblievat'* – to "water" the female relatives who are present. Water is the symbol of life and the pouring of water is a gesture meant to bestow year-long health and beauty. Some use a spray of perfume instead of water, or both. In return for the watering, the men are offered something to eat and a shot of strong alcohol. Younger boys in the party are sometimes given a decorated egg, chocolate, and/or money.

The "watering" has many forms and can range from a teaspoon of warm tap water to an entire bucket of cold well water.

In addition, there is the *šibat'*, which means to be lightly whipped with braided willow branches. This is a ritual that is also directed toward the females of the family. The willow branch is chosen because it is the first tree that 'wakes' in spring and, according to folk tradition, the fertility and vitality from the branches were thought to flow into the woman during this act.

It's not surprising to hear that many Slovak girls and women aren't exactly enthusiastic about Easter Monday and are often anxious about what they will encounter through the day.

Though most Slovak girls and women dislike some of these tradition today, this was not always the case in the past. Traditionally, in each village, the 'watering' and 'whipping' would be done by a group of single young men, who would decide among themselves which single young women they would visit. If the group left out a particular girl, it was a sign that none of the boys in the group had an interest in her. Therefore, some say that girls actually wanted to get watered and whipped.

Všetkých svätých **and** ***Dušičky*** – **All Saints' Day:** The holiday of All Saints' Day on November 1 is recognized as a national holiday in many European countries. On this day in Slovakia, people young and old go to cemeteries where loved ones are buried to pay their respects by bringing wreaths or flowers and lighting votive candles to leave on the gravestones. A few days before, a family member close to the deceased will have come to clean the grave site by doing things such as clearing away old flowers or leaves.

There is a steady number of visitors throughout All Saint's Day, but many people come in the late afternoon and early evening. Around this time it is getting dark and cemeteries take on a special quality, as they are filled with families and friends walking amongst the graves that are decorated with flowers and candles.

Vianoce – **Christmas:** Though the three days of December 24, 25, and 26 are designated as the Christmas holidays, most families celebrate the majority of festivities on December 24th with the traditional Christmas dinner followed by the attending of a church service in the evening (usually midnight mass). Gifts, which are said to be brought by *Ježiško* – the baby Jesus, and not Santa Claus—are exchanged and opened in the evening after dinner, either before or after attending church service. The traditional Christmas dinner may vary according to region but mainly consists of *kapustnica* – cabbage soup—with the main dish of *kapor* – carp fish and *zemiakový šalát* – potato salad.

A plate of medovníky - a kind of honey cookie that is popular at Christmas time

One of the important traditions that takes place before the meal is the sharing of the *oplátky* – unleavened wafers that are distributed when everyone is seated around the table. One usually puts *med* – or honey on the *oplátky,* and takes a piece of *cesnak* – or garlic to eat with the *oplátky* to symbolize a happy and healthy life during the year. Also, in many families an apple and walnuts are symbolically part of the pre-meal rituals. An apple is sliced down the middle horizontally and if the center, which should be in the shape of a star, is without any blemishes, then it is said that it will be a good year. A walnut or a few of them are cracked opened at the table with the hope that the quarter pieces inside are not shriveled. Each quarter represents a season of the year. Some families throw pieces of walnut into every corner of the room to symbolize giving food to the ghosts of their ancestors.

Silvester – **New Year's Eve:** People in Slovakia spend New Year's Eve much the same way people in other parts of the world do, with family or friends, at home or in the town. What is different from most Western traditions, however, is the restrictions of what should be eaten on New Year's Day. Usually, no poultry of any kind is eaten on this first day of the year, as it is said that anything with wings will fly away with your luck for the next year. Fish is usually eaten and it is said that if you take a single fish scale and put it in your purse or wallet, you will have fortune in the new year. And one more thing: in Slovakia you wish someone "Happy New Year" only after the new year has begun, beginning right after midnight.

Also, Slovaks say that what you do on the first day of the year will determine how you will be spending the whole year. As the expression says, *Ako na Nový rok, tak po celý rok* – How it is on New Year's day, it will be the whole year. So if you are lazy on the first of January and do nothing the whole day, you will also be doing nothing and be lazy throughout the whole year.

Additionally, Slovak independence is also celebrated on January 1. The Slovak Republic was established on January 1, 1993.

OTHER EVENTS

There are many other wonderful traditions observed throughout the seasons. In the month of May it's possible to see a maypole or two, particularly in the smaller towns and villages. As the tradition goes, a young single man who was interested in a particular young lady would put up a maypole in her yard as a two-fold symbol demonstrating his interest in her, as well as declaring that "she's taken." Though the tradition of the maypole is no longer interpreted as it once was, it is still a reminder of spring and commonly seen around towns and villages today.

A maypole in the garden of a cottage in Vlkolínec

The *jarmok* is something like a county fair that takes place in many towns in the late summer or early autumn around the time of the wine harvest. Many booths with items such as handmade crafts, rugs, wooden utensils, as well as traditional Slovak foods can be found alongside the more common goods such as plastic toys for children, cheaply manufactured clothing, or household items. The variety of items from one *jarmok* to another will vary, but almost all share one particularity: *burčiak*. *Burčiak* can be translated as 'new wine', which is the juice made from crushed grapes that is in the fermenting process but has not yet reached the stage where it can be classified as wine. *Burčiak* comes in both the red and white varieties. A word of caution: don't be fooled by the grape-juice taste. It doesn't taste like it's particularly strong but the effects are felt quickly.

In the areas of Slovakia that have a wine making tradition such as in the western towns of Pezinok and Modra, the festival known as *vinobranie* is just as popular. These festivals are also held, similarly to a *jarmok*, once a year around autumn time. But the festivities of a *vinobranie* are usually on a much larger scale with a greater variety of foods, traditional crafts, and entertainment.

In the last five years or so, western holidays such as Halloween and Valentine's Day have been introduced to Slovakia. Posters of flying witches, ghosts, and bright orange pumpkins can be seen in many shop windows in the weeks prior to October 31. Costumes and face paints are sold to encourage children to dress up for Halloween at school. The tradition of going trick-or-treating, however, has not been adopted. Many Slovaks are of the opinion that Halloween and Valentine's Day were introduced as money-making opportunities for retailers who sell everything from motif socks and underwear to heart-painted mugs and chocolate. And one final note about the commercialization of holidays: don't be surprised to see Christmas decorations in major department stores and malls go up in October as well as Christmas-themed commercials on TV, which start in early November.

NAME-DAYS AND LEGENDS

According to Slovak tradition, almost every day of the calendar year has a name or two (male, female, or both) assigned to it; for example, June 10th is the name-day for Margareta. The names are generally those of Catholic saints who have dates associated with them on the church calendar. Others are popular names that have been assigned a random date on the calendar.

A name-day is treated similarly to a birthday, being marked just slightly less in importance than a birthday. Usually on a name-day a close relative or a close friend might present the person with flowers or a small gift, possibly even a cake. In addition to this, the person is given a handshake, a kiss on both cheeks, and a wishing of *všetko najlepšie* – "all the best." For a colleague or someone that you don't know well, a simple handshake and the *všetko najlepšie* will suffice. There is usually no connection between someone's given name and the time of the year they were born. Someone can have a birthday and name-day in the same month or at opposite times of the year.

Over the centuries, during the times when country folk didn't have access to calendars or were unable to read, the name-days were used as a kind of marker of time through the year and short expressions or legends became attached to the names. For example, November 11 is the day of St. Martin. The pagan feast of the winter solstice began around this time. According to folk legend, it is said that "St. Martin came riding into town on his white horse" on that day, meaning that the snow season is marked to begin anytime from November 11 onward.

Another example of the link between nature and name-days is on May 12, 13, and 14, which are named for the saints Pankrác, Servác, and Bonifác, respectively. Up until this time of the year, the weather in spring is highly variable and the threat to crops from cold and frost is always present. It is said that Pankrác, Servác, and Bonifác are the "frozen men" who bring cold weather. According to the cycles of nature that had been observed, if it is freezing on these days, there will be a longer threat of cold weather and a greater possibility of damage to crops. If it doesn't freeze on these days, then the threat of continued frost is said to have passed.

Another important name-day is that of St. Mikuláš, on December 6. The night before, children clean their shoes and place them close to the door or on the window sill, in the hopes that if they have been good, Mikuláš will bring them a small gift, like tangerines, peanuts, or chocolate. If you were bad, you might get a lump of coal, an onion, or an old potato. Though this is similar to the story of St. Nicholas who is the original Santa Claus, the day of Mikuláš isn't necessarily connected with Christmas.

The names Adam and Eve are celebrated on December 24 and Štefan's day, another day of celebration and party, is on December 26. Also, the name Silvester is celebrated on December 31. Would it now make sense to you if someone asked you what plans you have for Silvester?

SEE MORE

Take a look at appendix E in the back of this book for the Slovak calendar of name-days to see if your name is there. If it isn't, pick one. It's a great excuse to get someone to take you out to lunch or to go for a drink with some friends.

Dancing under the maypole

CHAPTER

7

LEISURE AND RECREATION

THEATER, OPERA, AND MUSIC

There are 24 professional theaters supported by the state budget throughout Slovakia. The most important of these is the *Slovenské národné divadlo (SND)* – the Slovak National Theater—in Bratislava. The *Slovenské národné divadlo* is a repertory institution with permanent companies in opera, ballet, and drama. The season starts in September with performances everyday except for Sundays (for opera and ballet) and Mondays (for drama), until the end of June. Check their Web site, www.snd.sk, for a list of performances and the schedule.

There are two buildings that comprise the Slovak National Theater in Bratislava. One is the historic old theater on Hviezdoslav Square in the *Staré Mesto*, and the new national theater that recently opened in April 2007, located in the Nivy area, close to the Apollo bridge, also in Bratislava.

Below are names of professional theaters in other major cities and towns:

- Košice: *Štátne divadlo* – State Theater, www.sdke.box.sk
- Banská Bystrica: *Štátna opera a balet* – State Opera and Ballet, www.stateopera.sk
- Nitra: *Divadlo Andreja Bagara* – The Theater of Andrej Bagar, www.dab.sk

For most performances, reserving tickets in advance is recommended. Reservations can be made through the box office or through Ticket Portal, www.ticketportal.sk. Performances usually begin at 7:00 pm.

There are also some excellent musical orchestras. The most well known philharmonic orchestras are those of the Symphonic Orchestra of Bratislava, www.filharm.sk; the *Štátna filharmónia Košice* – the Slovak State Philharmonic in Košice, www.sfk.sk; and *Štátny komorný orchester Žilina* – the Slovak Sinfonietta of Žilina.

The National Theater in Bratislava

MUSEUMS, GALLERIES, AND CINEMAS

Slovakia has many significant museums. Here are some of the most well known:

- The Slovak National Museum in Bratislava, www.snm.sk
- The Slovak National Gallery in Bratislava, www.sng.sk
- The Slovak National Uprising Museum in Banská Bystrica, www.muzeumsnp.sk
- The Slovak National Ethnographic Museum in Martin, www.snm.sk
- The Slovak Mining Museum in Banská Štiavnica, www.muzeumbs.sk
- The Technical Museum in Košice, www.stm-ke.sk
- The Andy Warhol Museum in Medzilaborce

Bratislava has the greatest variety of museums and galleries in the entire country with new exhibits constantly changing. More detailed information on all Slovak museums can be found at www.muzeum.sk.

NOTE

Museums are usually closed on Mondays unless otherwise stated.

You can find a cinema in any town or city in Slovakia. With the arrival of malls and other large shopping areas in Bratislava, new movie theaters are being built in the style of the multiplexes so common elsewhere. Indeed, if you're sitting in a movie theater at the Polus shopping center in Bratislava, you could just as well be sitting at a movie theater in Norfolk, Virginia—the experience is the same. English language films are popular and screenings are usually with Slovak subtitles rather than dubbed. For information about theaters in Bratislava visit www.istropoliscinemacenter.sk and www.palacecinemas.sk.

NIGHTLIFE

Discovering night-time diversion in any part of the world depends significantly on your location and your interests. Of course, the variety of social activities and the number of each type of activity depends on whether the environment is urban or rural. Theoretically, a large city offers more options for social interaction than a small village, though this isn't always the case. Many social environments can be found across Slovakia, whether they be in the larger cosmopolitan cities such as Bratislava, Košice, or Banská Bystrica, or in a small village in the countryside.

Pubs / Bars – Pubs and bars vary by type and style, and cater to a range of clientele from the uptown set (what you would find in the center of the *Staré Mesto* – or Old Town in Bratislava, for example), to the average worker frequenting a local establishment. What may be tricky is figuring out the lingo for the various types of establishments, which serve, among other things, alcoholic beverages.

- *Bar* – Similar meaning as in English. A bar is a place that serves mainly alcoholic drinks including a wide variety of mixed drinks and hard alcohol.

- *Krčma* – A pub or tavern. A krčma often contains a bar and also serves food or light snacks, but usually nothing fancy.

- *Hostinec* – This word is not used often in spoken language but you might see it on the façade of an old building. The meaning is often used interchangeably with krčma. A hostinec would likely be found in a village or small town rather than in a city.

Historically, a hostinec used to refer to a place where travelers stayed overnight on their way to another destination. In a hostinec they would serve meals on the ground floor and have a few rooms for visitors on the floor(s) above. They were located either close to major roads or in smaller towns. Note the root-word 'host' in hostinec.

- *Vináreň* – wine bar—A place that specializes in the production and/or selling of wine, often located in a cellar.

- *Podnik* – A generic term used to mean any place where you can sit and order drinks and possibly a meal or snack. It could be a bar, restaurant, *vináreň*, etc.

The pub scene is an important part of Slovak culture.

Movies – Going to the movies on a Friday or Saturday night is standard almost everywhere. In the summer, many Slovaks enjoy viewing a movie in an outdoor amphitheater. Many towns have one, and being outdoors at the movies with friends is a welcomed summer diversion.

Music and Dance – Music, clubbing and dancing are other parts of nightlife that will vary according to location. The cities have a greater number of clubs and discotheques, with a variety of music genres to choose from. A dance club called *Subclub* in Bratislava for example, www.subclub.sk, featuring electronica and live concerts. At the other end of the spectrum, going to a 'disco' in a village or small town could mean that the majority of people are ages 16 and younger, dancing to pop tunes.

OUTDOOR ACTIVITIES

Slovakia offers a variety of opportunities for outdoor activities. If you are interested in winter snow sports, more than 30 mountain regions offer great opportunities for downhill and cross-country skiing, as well as snowboarding. The best locations are probably in the Tatra Mountains where snow is on the ground for an average of 130 days out of the year. The best known ski slopes in the High Tatras are around the towns of Štrbské Pleso, Starý and Nový Smokovec, Tatranská Lomnica, and Ždiar. These tend to get crowded over the Christmas and Easter holidays. Other popular areas outside of the Tatras are the Slovenský Raj range, the Malá Fatra range, and Vrátna Dolina.

Information about the slopes, conditions, and ski resorts can be found at www.ski.sk, and www.holidayinfo.sk.

SEE MORE

As more foreign tourists have become aware of Slovakia's magnificent mountains, many ski resorts, particularly in the Tatras, have been steadily increasing their prices, making a holiday there more difficult for the average Slovak to afford. In addition to this, many Slovaks comment that the quality of the services offered has not improved with the increase in prices. Though this may be true, many hotels are going through renovations and making changes to meet the expectations of foreign visitors.

The warmer seasons also support a good variety of sports and recreation. If you love the Tatras in the winter, you might return there in the summer for some hiking excursions. All mountain areas have a good network of marked trails, and with a decent map (which isn't difficult to find), it's easy to plan a hike in advance. Spending the night in a *chata* – cottage—along the routes is an option you may consider to further the experience of living in a mountain wilderness. Unfortunately, the multitudes of fellow hikers who tend to crowd the Tatras in the summer may detract from any romantic notion you have of nature and solitude.

SEE MORE

For more information about points of interest in the Tatras, check out www.tatry.net, www.tatry.org, or www.vysoke-tatry.sk.

If the Tatras are not to your taste, try Slovenský raj, www.slovenskyraj.sk; a national park in the central-eastern region of the country. The name translates to Slovak Paradise, and it will become apparent why it is named so when you make your way through the valleys and canyons. Chains and ladders are made available to safely lead hikers through gorges and near by waterfalls. To some this may sound a bit too adventurous, but in reality, you don't have to be a serious hiker to enjoy Slovenský raj. In addition to the amazing hikes, the park has a high number of plant species as well as a variety of wild animals, from bats that live in the caves to European wild cats.

If you are interested in cycling, there are a few cycling routes in Slovakia worth mentioning. Europe's longest cycling route from Passau, Germany, to Budapest, Hungary, goes along the Danube River through Vienna and Bratislava. Another cycling route in the Bratislava area is the Morava-Danube route, which starts on the left bank of the Danube under the New Bridge and heads up to the area of Devín. In the east of Slovakia, a 40-kilometer cycling route close to

Košice called the Hornád (named after the local river), is noteworthy, and future plans will connect this route across the Hungarian border with an existing route in Hungary.

Joggers getting some exercise in the afternoon

Swimming is a popular activity in Slovakia, particularly in the summer. The larger towns and cities have several indoor swimming pools but they vary in quality. A few aquatic centers have begun to pop up across the country with more planned for the future. Aquapark Tatralandia is three kilometers from Liptovský Mikuláš and is the largest aquatic center in Slovakia. It boasts six swimming pools filled with water from thermal springs. Aquapark Poprad has four pools, two indoor and two outdoor. Bratislava Aupark Aulandia is located in Petržalka on the second floor of the shopping mall Aupark.

Other sporting interests that are actively pursued in Slovakia are tennis, www.tenis.sk or www.tenisclub.sk; horseback riding, www.horses.sk; canoeing, www.swim.sk; white water rafting, and mountain climbing. Golf is a sport that is growing in popularity in Slovakia, with a few courses located throughout the country. Sites include Bernolákovo, which is close to Bratislava, www.golf.sk; Tále, near Brezno in the Low Tatras, www.graybear.sk; and Alpinka in Košice.

PLACES OF INTEREST

Spas—The abundance of natural thermal springs throughout Slovakia has contributed to a spa tradition that goes back centuries. Slovaks hold a strong belief in the therapeutic powers of these spas, proven by centuries of custom and by thousands of foreign patients who regularly return for spa treatments. One may spend several weeks at a spa undergoing treatment and physical therapy for a specific ailment. Professional medical staff is on hand to treat a variety of ailments ranging from arthritis to more complex conditions. Usually, each spa specializes in the treatment of certain ailments. For example, the spa at Piešťany is famous for treatment of locomotive organs and osteoporosis. Other spas are famous for the treatment of the digestive tract and metabolic disorders, cardiovascular diseases, and so on.

In addition to this traditional use of spas, more and more spa centers are working to draw the interest of patrons through tourism. Many of the more well-known spas such as those in Piešťany or Trenčianske Teplice attract visitors who are interested in short 2-3 day visits for recreational purposes. These previously mentioned locations have excellent spa facilities and are surrounded by beautiful countryside, which encourages other outdoor activities such as walking, hiking, or cycling during warmer weather, and skiing in the nearby hills and mountains in the winter.

Caves—Slovakia has several thousand caves, but because of their delicate nature and the interest in long term preservation, only a few are accessible to the public. Those caves that are open to the public are examples of some of nature's most unique scenery.

Two general areas in Slovakia contain these vast networks of caves. The *Kras* – or Karst region—located southwest of Košice, contains the popular *Domica*, one of the better known caves. The Karst region spans across parts of Slovakia and Hungary, and both nations have declared their regions protected. UNESCO, an organization dedicated to the preservation and restoration of sites of historic or natural significance, has also bestowed this region with World Heritage Site status.

The second area of caves is located beneath the Low Tatras. Here, the most famous caves are *Demänovská ľadová jaskyňa* – Demänovská Ice Cave, and *Demänovská jaskyňa slobody* – Demänovská Freedom Cave. Another important cave that should be mentioned is the *Dobšinská ľadová jaskyňa* – Dobšinská Ice Cave—located south of Poprad, which also has status as a World Heritage Site under UNESCO.

For information on Slovak caves, a good Web site is www.ssj.sk. It contains information about all the caves in Slovakia, those that are accessible to the public, access information, and opening hours. Unfortunately the Web site is in Slovak only; hopefully this will change.

Historic Towns—A pleasant way to spend a day or a weekend is to take a train to one of the country's many historic towns and do a little exploring on your own. It can be quite exciting to do some research on a town, experiment with the public transportation, photograph whatever strikes your fancy, and eat in a local restaurant. Slovakia has many such towns and villages that are definitely worth the trip. Depending on your desired travel time and where you are in the country, you can find an interesting destination as close as a half hour away.

For example, located just 20 minutes outside of Bratislava is the village of Svätý Jur. This small village has still intact portions of a seventeenth–century wall that once surrounded the village for the purpose of keeping out the

Turks. Also, there is a castle ruin called *Biely kameň* – White Stone—which is a short hike into the woods above the village but worth the climb if you're interested.

So many fascinating historical and cultural relics are tucked away in the Slovak countryside that it's an injustice to name just a few. The best advice is to talk to locals who know the surrounding areas better than anything you might read. Do the research, get out there, and discover the country!

Castles and Ruins—In addition to historic towns, numerous castles and ruins are just waiting to be explored. Castles that are intact such as Bratislava Castle, Orava Castle, or Bojnice Castle, have museums or exhibits that provide the history of the castle. One of the most visited and well preserved castles in east Slovakia is Krásna Hôrka, www.hradkrasnahorka.sk

Orava Castle

Castle ruins, on the other hand, arise out of the landscape, most without accompanying informational postings or guides. Although they are a bit more secretive about their historic past, they leave the door wide open for your imagination to reconstruct and envision just where you'd store the provisions or place the archers.

Many ruins have been left unattended for centuries after being destroyed by fires or by invaders from the Turks to Napoleon. Slovakia's most famous ruins are *Devínsky hrad* – Devín Castle—located just outside of Bratislava, and *Spišský hrad* – Spiš Castle—which is also the largest ruin in Central Europe.

A good starting point may be the Web site www.castles.sk. It contains basic information about all castles in Slovakia, approximately 250. The Web site also contains a map of Slovak historic regions with links to information on specific castles and ruins in the region.

Wooden Churches—Among the remaining legacies of the Rusyn people of Eastern Slovakia are the wooden churches that are located in the north-eastern portion of the country. They are a unique asset to Slovak heritage. There are 27 protected wooden churches in all, mostly located in small villages. Most of these churches date back to the eighteenth century, but the oldest church, located in Hervartov, was built around 1500. These churches are primarily Byzantine Catholic, with many still serving their official function as places of worship.

UNESCO Sites—Since Slovakia's independence in 1993, the country has had six official entries accepted into the list of world culture and natural heritage under UNESCO:

- The town of Banská Štiavnica
- The village of Vlkolínec, which is a historical preservation of folk architecture
- Spišský Castle, the largest castle ruin in all of Central Europe
- The town of Bardejov, which has a Medieval historic center
- Dobšinská ľadová jaskyňa, ice cave
- The caves of the Slovak Karst

SEASONAL EVENTS

Slovaks enjoy an array of distinct and exciting events throughout the year. Below is a list of some of the better-known seasonal events.

SPRING

- Festival of Ghosts and Spirits at Bojnice Castle— weekends in late April and early May, www.bojnicecastle.sk
- Dobrofest in Trnava—four days over the first weekend in June, www.dobrofest.sk. This country music (American) and dance festival is a tribute to the memory of John Dopyera, a Slovak-American inventor of the resophonic dobro, an acoustic guitar produced with metal resonators to amplify sound.

SUMMER

- International festival of folk costume-dressed dolls—the first weekend in June. The *Medzinárodný festival krojovaných bábik* is a children's festival that takes place in Kežmarok.
- Myjava Folk Festival—the third weekend in June in the town of Myjava. The first major folk dance festival of the summer with a nice display of handicrafts.
- *Zamagurské folklórne slávnosti*—a "folklore celebration" that takes place in the village of Červený Kláštor the third weekend in June.
- Art Film Festival in Trenčianske Teplice—One week in June in the beautiful spa town of Trenčianske Teplice, www.artfilm.sk. This is Slovakia's biggest film festival.
- Summer Drama and Opera Festival in Zvolen—two and a half weeks in June, www.djgt.sk. The festival takes place in the courtyard at Zvolen castle.
- Eurofolklore in Banská Bystrica—an international folklore festival the last weekend in June.

- Cassovia Folkfest in Košice—an extended weekend the fourth week in June, www.folkfest.sk. The folkfest includes handicrafts, food, music, and folk dancing.

- Folk Festival Východná—First weekend in July. This three-day festival features only the very best performers in folk dance and music and has a great international presence as well.

- Pilgrimage to the Virgin Mary—the first weekend in July. This is the largest pilgrimage of the year for Catholics and takes place in Levoča where up to 250,000 people make their way to the small church overlooking the town.

- Folk Festival under Poľana, Detva—the second weekend in July, www.detva.sk. The theme of this festival is the music and dance of the famous region of Detva.

- The International Festival of Handicrafts in Kežmarok—the second weekend in July. This festival highlights the tradition of handcrafted goods.

- Pohoda Festival in Trenčín—A weekend in mid-July, www.pohodafestival.sk. Slovakia's largest open air music festival, which usually features more than 130 Slovak and international bands and performers.

- Jánošík's Days International Folk Festival in Terchová—the first weekend in August.

- International Festival of Historical Fencing at Spiš Castle—July or August, www.spisskyhrad.sk. This is an annual event that features performances from fencing groups.

FALL/WINTER

- Vinobranie—various weeks in September in wine growing areas (particularly Pezinok and Modra). This festival is held once a year in the autumn, around the time of grape harvesting for making wine. A vinobranie is usually on a large scale with a variety of foods, traditional crafts, and entertainment.

- Košice Peace Marathon—the first Saturday in October, www.mmm.sk. The *Medzinárodný maratón mieru* – International Peace Marathon, has been an annual event since 1924 and is the oldest running uninterrupted marathon in Europe.

- International Festival of Mountain Films in Poprad—the second weekend in October, www.mfhf.sk. This four-day event features an international collection of films and documentaries on sports and nature.

- The Days of the Košice Folk Ensembles—the second or third week of November. This event, *Dni košických folklórnych súborov,* brings together all folk ensembles in Košice to give several joint performances throughout the week. There also is a *škola tanca* – or dance school—where certified dance instructors teach basic steps from a particular folk region.

- Christmas Market—usually begins the last weekend in November or the first weekend in December, and lasts until December 23. The *Vianočný trh* – or Christmas Market—takes place in all of the larger towns throughout Slovakia. They include handmade arts and crafts, a good variety of foods, and a great Christmas atmosphere. Don't forget to have a hot cup of *medovina* – honey wine, *varené víno* – mulled wine that comes in red or white varieties, or *punč* – basically fruit juice mixed with rum—to keep you smiling and warm through the night.

SEE MORE

For more information or a list of other events, see the following Web sites: www.kultura.sk, www.divadlo.sk, www.slovakspectator.sk under the cultural section; www.slovakiatourism.sk, and www.panorama.sk/calendar for a list of events happening in Bratislava.

FOOD AND DRINK

TYPICAL SLOVAK FOODS

Slovak cuisine is not something that can be defined by national borders. Often a 'typical' meal in one country (goulash, for example) is almost the same 'typical' meal that is prepared in its neighboring country or countries. It would be more appropriate to define cuisine by regions rather than physical borders. Just as western Slovakia is influenced by and has influenced its Austrian and Czech neighbors, eastern Slovakia, Ukraine, Poland, and Hungary all influence one another.

The most commonly prepared meat in Slovak dishes is pork. A typical plate would be a pork cutlet, breaded and fried, served with potato salad. In Austria this cutlet is called *schnitzel* where as in Slovakia it's called *vyprážaný bravčový rezeň*. Dishes prepared with beef such as *stejk* – steak—are not as common as pork and would be rather more expensive than pork when ordered in a restaurant. Chicken is another popular choice and is preferred by many over pork. It is also a food prepared internationally and therefore many tasty variations are easier to come by.

Slovak food is often described as "stick-to-your-ribs fare" that doesn't tend to follow today's emphasis on healthy eating. Slovak food isn't generally 'unhealthy' but if you have specific dietary needs, make allowances for the way some foods are prepared. For example, when possible, request having your main course baked not fried, and watch the butter. Slovaks, tend to eat lots of fresh fruits and vegetables in their daily living (often grown in their own gardens) but you aren't likely to see a big choice of fruit or vegetable dishes offered in restaurants.

Lunch at the university: rezeň, boiled potatoes, and pickles

Soups are generally light but are an important part of daily meals, eaten either before lunch or dinner. Soups can be categorized as *kyslá* – sour—meaning that they are made with milk or cream but not necessarily sour in taste, or *sladká* – sweet—which doesn't mean that they are sweet but that they are water–based. In east Slovakia cream-based soups are also called *podbitá* soups. In contrast, stews are thicker and eaten as a full meal with bread. There are many varia-tions of *guláš* – goulash (which is known internationally mostly as a Hungarian dish because it is seasoned with paprika)—that are typically prepared with pork. One popular cabbage *guláš* made with pork and boiled with cream is *segedínsky guláš* and is typically served with *knedľa* – slices of a soft bread that is steamed rather than baked.

Vegetarian dishes are slowly making their way onto menus and into people's vocabularies. Declaring *"Som vegetarián(ka)"* – "I'm a vegetarian"—hardly creates the stir that it once would have but finding a meatless meal can still be a challenge at times. Often the only vegetarian dish on menus, particularly outside of bigger towns, might be fried cheese with french fries – *vyprážaný syr s hranolkami*.

Parené buchty is another common meal made from a flour-based dough and filled with a fruit or berry jam. These are covered with a mix of cocoa powder and powdered sugar.

Still, it's good to know that a significant portion of Slovak cuisine is flour-based, for example *palacinky* – thin pancakes with various fruit fillings. These are sometimes covered with a chocolate sauce and whipped cream that can be served as a main course, not just a dessert. There's also *pirohy* – boiled dumplings filled with potato and/or cheese. *Pirohy* are usually covered with cheese and served with a sprinkle of bacon on top, so if you don't want it served to you this way, order it *bez slaniny* – without bacon. In east Slovakia, particularly in the Zemplín region, *pirohy* are made with sweet fillings; *slivkový lekvár* – plum jam—is the most common. These *pirohy "nasladko"* – sweet *pirohy*—are topped with sugar, roast bread crumbs, and melted butter, and are served as a main course.

The national dish of Slovakia is called *bryndzové halušky*, a dish that is probably unlike anything you've had before if you're not familiar with the food of this region. *Halušky* are made from a flour-based dough combined with grated potato, and then cut in small pieces that are boiled. The *halušky* are served topped with crumbled *bryndza* – a soft sheep's cheese—and bits of bacon. *Bryndzové halušky* may not sound too appetizing according to the description, but it's a treat, particularly if you are a dairy lover. The meal is often served with milk, which complements the meal superbly. Any traditional Slovak restaurant worth its salt will have this national dish on the menu.

Another meal that is typically Slovak, though more popular in the east of the country, is *holúbky* – stuffed cabbage. Ground pork meat and rice with tomato sauce are rolled into steamed cabbage leaves. These stuffed cabbage leaves are then stewed until the contents are cooked.

A beverage that should be mentioned as typically Slovak is a soft drink called *kofola*. *Kofola* was an invention of a Czechoslovak research institute in the 1960s. It combines such flavors as roasted coffee grounds, cinnamon, coriander, and caramel. Though it's comparable to a kind of root-beer, it has a unique, somewhat bitter, herbal flavor that you might not take to at first. Kofola is best when served directly from the tap. It is particularly popular during the summer when a cool drink is welcome.

THE AVAILABILITY OF FRESH FOODS

With Slovakia continuing its transition into a market economy as well as accession into the EU, European-based supermarket chains have been expanding throughout the country. In the past, the availability of fresh fruits and vegetables was contingent upon local seasonal yields and in the winter, for example, the selection was uninspiring. These days, with major international supermarket chains reasonably well dispersed, a year-round selection of even the more exotic fruits and vegetables, like avocado or mango, is becoming standard.

In addition to the grocery stores, be sure to check out the farmer's markets that can be found in almost every town or city. You can usually find the best deals and freshest produce on hand, and at the same time support the local community through your purchases of a wide variety of fruits and vegetables, nuts or honey.

Low-fat milk and a variety of breads

Fresh breads are easy to come by and in every city, town, and village there is a *pekáreň* – bakery or *potraviny* – grocery store—that sells fresh bread. There is usually a very good variety to choose from, but the most common loaf breads are *čierny* – black and *biely* – white bread. Also very common are the long rolls called *rožky*, and the round rolls called *žemle*.

The most common kind of milk found in Slovakia is *trvanlivé mlieko* – long-lasting milk. This milk is sold in a one-liter cardboard carton and not refrigerated until after opening. The main varieties are *plnotučné* – full fat, consisting of 3.5% milk fat, *polotučné* – half fat, consisting of 1.5% milk fat, and *nízkotučné* – low fat, consisting of .5% milk fat. *Vysokopasterizované mlieko* – high-pasteurized milk—is also available, though not as popular, and can usually be found in the refrigerated section near the yogurt and butter.

COFFEE AND TEA

Coffee drinkers around the world share an international language of terms for the different kinds of preparations of coffee. These terms are based on the Italian names that have become standard, such as espresso, cappuccino, or caffe latte. Many upscale restaurants and cafés in Slovakia may have an entire coffee menu entirely with these Italian names.

Other types of coffee commonly found in a Slovak menu are the following: *Presso* – espresso made from a "Presso" machine, and *zalievaná káva* – coffee made by pouring boiling water over loose grounds. After the latter is served in a cup, wait a few minutes for the grounds to settle before drinking. This is also called *turecká káva*, which translates to "Turkish coffee." *Viedenská káva* – Viennese coffee—is coffee with whipped cream and *alžírska kava* – Algerian coffee—is coffee with eggnog.

Instant coffee is commonly prepared at home. It can be called *instantná káva,* but more often this kind of coffee is called *neska,* named for the brand which is a household name: Nescafé®.

For tea drinkers, there are usually the following to choose from: *čierny čaj* – black tea, *zelený čaj* – green tea, *ovocný čaj* – fruit tea, or *bylinkový čaj* – herbal tea.

Alcohol: Beer, Wine and the Harder Stuff

To a large extent, Central and Eastern Europeans, particularly Russians, are stereotyped as being heavy drinkers of hard alcohol. Hard alcohol certainly has its place in Slovakia, but that isn't to say that other kinds of alcohol are completely ignored. In Slovakia, there is also a long tradition of brewing excellent beers and making very respectable wines, particularly white wines, in Slovakia.

Many people enjoy beer. It is often an essential beverage for socializing at pubs and bars. For some, learning how to say *"jedno pivo, prosím"* – "one beer, please"—ranks high on the list with *"kde je záchod?"* – "where's the bathroom?"—as important phrases to memorize.

When you order a beer, the person taking your order is going to want to know your preference: *tmavé* – dark or *svetlé* – light (color), and also *malé* – small or *veľké* – large—three deciliters or half a liter. Dark beers are usually sweeter than the more bitter light-colored beers. Slovakia is an established producer of quality beers, but famous beers from the Czech Republic are also available at some restaurants and pubs.

Many Slovak beers are influenced by the pilsner kinds of beers. Remember that western Slovakia borders the Czech Republic, which is the beer drinking capital of the world. There is such a great variety of Slovak brands alone without considering Czech or German beers. The following columns of beer brands are the more popular for dark and light beers (not in any particular order):

Dark	Light
Šariš	Zlatý Bažant
Stein	Kelt
Topvar	Steiger
Corgoň	Budvar

Many brands have both light and dark varieties. It's simply a matter of taste, and if you are a beer drinker you'll certainly look forward to conducting your own survey. Beer is a favorite among college students because it is cheaper than most other alcoholic beverages. Often times beer is also cheaper than non-alcoholic drinks such as bottled mineral water or soda. The average price for a large beer in Bratislava, which is probably the highest priced in Slovakia but still considerably cheap, is approximately €.90, or $1.21 USD (30Skk) to €1.20, or $1.61 USD (40Skk).

In the western region of Slovakia, along the foothills of the Lesser Carpathian Mountains, wine is the alcoholic beverage of choice. In this region lies the historically important Pentapolitana wine district, which is made up of the five wine growing areas of Bratislava, Svätý Jur, Pezinok, Modra, and Trnava. In this area of Slovakia, wine is at the center of several festivals and special events, most significant of which is the *vinobranie* – wine harvesting. In the wine town of Pezinok, for example, a pleasant evening can be spent at a restaurant or *vináreň* – wine cellar—enjoying some of the many excellent quality wines that are produced locally.The other important wine region that must be mentioned is the region of Tokaj located in the southeast, bordering with Hungary. In this case, the word 'region' should be stressed because the Tokaj brand name is used by both Hungarian and Slovak producers.

"Nazdravie", the equivalent to "cheers", literally means "To your health."

Many Slovaks grow fruit to produce their own wines and spirits. It's a source of pride to be able to serve a product that has come from one's own labor. Strong spirits can be distilled from many fruits; the most common are *slivovica,* made from plums, and *borovička*, made from juniper berries, *jablkovica* from apples, as well as *páleno* or *pálenka,* which is distilled from any mixed fruit.

If you are invited as a guest into someone's home, the chances are that, as a foreigner treated as an honored guest, you may be asked by your host(s) to join them in a toast of *slivovica* or *borovička* to welcome you. It could also be the case that it's 9 o'clock in the morning! The situation can prove to be sticky if you don't want to or can't drink alcohol. The bare minimum that is expected of you is to accept one toast, and generally then your hosts will feel they have satisfied their customary duty. But if you say no, for whatever reason, be ready to be pressured to change your mind. The trick is to be convivial yet firm in your decision. It is customary, especially among older generations, to decline once or twice and accept by the third offer. If you decline the third offer, this should be accepted (hopefully). Other good excuses to avoid drinking is to say that you are taking antibiotics, you are allergic to alcohol, or that you are driving.

Here are a few other tips to remember when involved in social drinking:

- When you are toasting, it is very important that you make eye contact with the person you are clinking glasses with. If you don't, you may be thought to be insincere.

- A common phrase equivalent to the English toast of "cheers" is *Na zdravie*, which literally means "To your health."

- Non-alcoholic drinks are not usually worthy of toasting status, and if you have a non-alcoholic drink you might not be asked to participate in a toast.

EATING OUT

Dining out doesn't hold as much cultural significance in Slovakia as it does in other European countries such as France or Italy, for example. Over the last several years, wage earners have begun to accrue a greater disposable income. As a result, the restaurant industry has seen an increase in the number of Slovaks who are interested in dining out for the simple pleasure of it and the quality in restaurants has increased to meet the expectations of customers looking for more than basic fare and basic service. Still, most Slovaks don't dine out. Food in a restaurant isn't typically exciting; it's a cost that most would rather forego, and it wouldn't usually be much better than what could be eaten at home.

That being said, for Slovaks, lunch is the main meal of the day and eating out for lunch is more common than for dinner, particularly for the working. Typical lunch eateries that cater to average workers include the *bufet* and *jedáleň*, which are more like cafeterias. At a *lahôdky* – delicatessen— you can find items such as ready-made sandwiches of salami, cheese, and egg. The pricing at all three kinds of eateries is fairly cheap. Also, for those who are on a tight monetary and/or time budget, the *bagetéria* – a shop that sells sandwiches made from baguettes—has increased in popularity and numerous ones have recently begun springing up in many locations.

Pizza—a common fast food choice

Many "fast food" kiosks sell foods such as hotdogs, hamburgers, pizza, and *hranolky* – french fries. If you buy a hamburger, it is most likely going to be a "ham" burger rather than a beef burger. Also, a cheeseburger usually comes with cheese only. Another typical fast food item is *langoš*. *Langoš* is a salted flour dough that is fried and then topped with any of the following: garlic, sour cream, ketchup or cheese. It's, well—greasy, but so delicious.

If you would like to have something more traditional than lunch on the go, many restaurants post the "specials" of the day, which attract mainly average office workers.

When dining at a restaurant and you ask for water with your meal, you are likely to be served *minerálna voda* – mineral water. If you'd prefer water without the bubbles, this is *nesýtená voda* or also called *neperlivá voda*. Both are sold in bottles. Your other option for plain water is a glass of *čistá voda* – tap water.

NOTE

If you order "just water" you will most likely get a glass or a small bottle of mineral water and you will have to pay for it.

Salads on a restaurant menu don't typically consist of a lettuce salad, though this is changing. Depending where you are in Slovakia, lettuce is not always readily available and you might be served a salad made with cabbage instead. Other kinds of fresh salads that are common are thinly sliced cucumber or tomato wedges in a lightly-sweetened vinaigrette.

NOTE

Side dishes don't always come automatically with a main course and may need to be ordered additionally.

Dining out in Slovakia is relatively affordable. At a nice restaurant you can expect to pay about €3.55, or $4.84 USD (120 Skk) to €4.75, or $6.45 USD (160 Skk) per person for a dinner meal. €7.50 or $10.10 USD (250 Skk) is expensive for a full meal at an average pub or restaurant. Restaurants may or may not accept credit cards as a form of payment, so be sure to ask in advance. Also, euros are not commonly accepted in restaurants, although this, too, might change as Slovakia moves closer to adopting the euro currency.

When paying at a restaurant or bar, the most common practice is to round up the bill. You will need to do some quick calculating and, if your total for example is €3.30, or

$4.50 USD (111 Skk) then you would probably pay €3.50, or $4.80 USD (120 Skk). At the time the waiter brings the bill, commonly, he or she waits to be paid on the spot. If you are handing the money to the waiter and say *Ďakujem, to je v poriadku* – thank you, that's ok—he or she won't give you back any change. If you don't say anything, he or she will give you back change. It isn't customary to leave a tip on the table before you leave. As a matter of fact, tipping the usual 10–20 percent of the price of the meal as is customary in the United States, for example, is not expected at all. Still, it is a habit that I have kept, knowing that waiters and waitresses work hard for low wages. So, in the case of the bill for €3.30, or $4.50 USD (111 Skk) I would probably pay €4.00, or $5.45 USD (135 Skk).

In many smaller villages outside of major tourist areas or away from main roads and highways, there might be no places to eat at all. There is a *krčma* – pub—in each village, but most likely they serve only drinks and some snacks at most, such as potato chips or pretzels. Another option may be to put together a meal from the choices in a *potraviny* – a small grocery store—with items such as bread, cheese, and yogurt.

In some bigger villages you may find a *bufet* or *lahôdky* – delicatessen. In places such as these there is no wait service. Usually you need to buy your food and pay for it at the counter, and then take it to a table or counter yourself. If you are in a small town and starving, and you can't find anything or everything is closed, look for a train or bus station. Most stations have either a *bufet* or a sandwich kiosk. Just don't expect anything fancy.

SEE MORE

For finding out what kinds of restaurants to choose from in Bratislava and other cities, or to see a sample menu, a good Web site is www.menu.sk, which has an English language version.

SOCIAL AND BUSINESS CUSTOMS

You might assume that the local customs in Slovakia are the same as in other European counties, but this isn't entirely the case. For example, did you know that the custom of 'ladies first' that is so common in many other cultures doesn't always apply in Slovakia? It is thought that a man should enter into an unfamiliar environment first before the woman just in case there should be something unsettling or dangerous going on. Or how about if you are standing in a crosswalk waiting to cross the street, an approaching car must stop to let you pass. Though this may be standard in Austria or Germany, you may be risking your life if you walk into the street expecting cars to stop for you.

BASIC GREETINGS

When making new acquaintances and introducing yourself either in a social or business setting, you can't go wrong with the simple handshake. A handshake is a safe bet, especially if you are aware that Slovaks frequently greet each other with the continental kiss on both cheeks but you aren't quite sure you understand exactly when it's appropriate. The greeting kiss is reserved for relatives or close friends with whom a closer relationship is shared. When meeting someone for the first time, a polite thing to say while exchanging a handshake is *teší ma* – nice to meet you.

NOTE When shaking hands, it is important that your hand is bare without a glove. To leave your gloves on is considered rude. The only exception is for a lady in an evening dress when gloves are part of the dress.

If you want to greet someone with a simple 'hello', there are a couple of choices. First is the ever popular *dobrý deň* – good day. This would be something you say to a shop assistant as you walk into a store or to a person you pass on the stairs on the way to your flat. When greeting a schoolmate or a colleague whom you see frequently and are on friendly terms with, the casual *čau* (plural, *čaute*), and *ahoj* (plural, *ahojte*) – hi—are good greetings and are used for both a hello and a good bye.

AN INVITATION TO SOMEONE'S HOME

Being invited to someone's home for a meal should be considered an honor. Slovaks are generally very generous hosts and treat their guests with respect. It's a nice gesture to bring something with you for your hosts when possible. Some ideas are a bottle of wine, a desert item such as a small cake or a choice of pastries, or chocolate. Upon arrival to someone's home, you will be expected to take off your shoes and usually offered a pair of *papuče* – slippers. This is a standard custom that you will find across Slovakia, so remember to put on a pair of decent looking socks before your visit.

If you've been invited for dinner it's likely you will be offered wine or another type of alcohol. If there is alcohol at the table, eating begins after the toast. Everyone usually stands for a toast and don't forget to make eye contact during this honored tradition! Only after you are sitting once again and someone says *Dobrú chuť* – Bon appetite— and everyone answers similarly, can you begin eating. Try to finish everything that is on your plate. Sometimes that can seem like quite a feat, especially if you don't particularly like something you've been served, but wasting food is something that is frowned upon. You may be offered a second serving, which you are free to turn down, but you probably shouldn't accept it unless you think you can finish it.

A typical first course is chicken soup with "rezance," a Slovak pasta noodle.

Flowers can be brought when invited to someone's home, for a birthday or other celebratory occasions, but it's important to keep a few tips in mind when buying them.

- Always choose an odd number of flowers, as even number bouquets are reserved for funerals.

- Most flowers have no significant meaning associated with them except for carnations and chrysanthemums, which are, again, more common for funerals.

- If the flowers are wrapped in paper from the flower shop, be sure to remove the paper before presenting the flowers.

A FEW NOTES ON BUSINESS ETIQUETTE

English as a business language is becoming increasingly important not only as a means for Slovaks to communicate with British and North American business clients but as the international language spoken between, for example, French or Italian business associates and their counterparts in Slovakia. Many Slovak companies have English speakers among their top managers and require English as a basic, necessary skill in hiring new employees. That being said, many contacts at Slovak companies are not fluent English speakers, and business representatives should be prepared to do business through translators. Also, it is often the case that office secretaries or telephone operators speak no English at all. In such cases, communication through e-mail or fax is an attractive alternative.

As stated earlier, a handshake is standard in either social or business settings, but don't forget to take off your gloves if you are wearing any. When being introduced to someone in a business setting, it is fine to either say *Teší ma* – Nice to meet you—and your last name or simply state your last name without saying any other greeting. Eye contact is important during the introduction and should be maintained the entire time that someone is addressing you.

Generally, Slovaks are more comfortable with being introduced by a third party rather than speaking up to introduce themselves directly. If after a few minutes no introduction is made, you can go ahead and introduce yourself.

Like many other Indo-European languages, the Slovak language has a formal and informal method of address. The formal *Vy* – you (formal) is used instead of the more familiar *ty* – you (informal). In the business environment the formal method of address is strictly applied, particularly with older generations or between older and younger employees. Usually the person with a higher rank, the person who is older, or a woman, may indicate to the younger or lower-ranked employee that they might speak to each other in the informal. Sometimes it's possible for employees to go several months or even years before saying, *Mohli by sme si potykať* – We could speak to each other in the informal.

Titles are more important in the written form than the spoken form unless one has the title of doctor; thus most people are either *pán* – mister, *pani* – misses, or *slečna* – miss, and their last name. Married women usually take their husband's last name but change the ending by adding a suffix, most commonly –ová but sometimes –á, depending on the spelling of name. For example the name *Minár* becomes *Minárová*.

Other titles you may see written before or after a person's name include the following:

Table 15: Academic titles

Mgr.	"Magister" – Master's degree in humanities, law, natural sciences, or performing arts.
Ing.	"Engineer" – Master's degree in a technical, agricultural, or economic discipline.
MSc.	"Master's of Science" – General Master's degree title that incorporates both Mgr. and Ing. titles. This title is not used as a written title.
JUDr.	"Doctor of Law" – Master's in Law with additional years of specified study.
MUDr.	"Doctor of Medicine" – Master's in Medicine.
PhDr.	This title is no longer awarded but was bestowed for studies achieved between a Master's degree and a PhD.
CSc.	"Candidate of Sciences" – A title which is no longer awarded, having the equivalent to a PhD.
PhD.	"Doctor of Philosophy" – Has the same usage as in English.
Doc.	"Docent" – Academic title of associate professor. Reached after completing the PhD., additional study, and publications.
DrSc.	"Doctor of Science" – The highest scientific degree reached by outstanding research work.
Prof.	"Professor" – The highest academic degree that can be achieved. The title *profesor* can only be granted by the President of Slovakia.

SOME FINAL WORDS OF ADVICE FOR SETTLING IN AND ADAPTING TO SLOVAK LIFE

Here are some last observations and pieces of advice for making your transition to Slovakia and its culture:

Bratislava has the potential to be disappointing if you come with the expectation of finding another Prague or Budapest; Bratislava will almost always suffer by comparison. If you are going to live in Bratislava, you personally will have to discover what you like and don't like about the city regardless of what you might have heard from others. Also remember that it's a good idea to travel outside of Bratislava to get the full scope and impression of the entire country.

Register at your local embassy. In addition to your embassy knowing about your presence, they can send you information about upcoming major events, how to vote absentee for elections, or who to contact if you need a new international driver's permit. All in all, it's nice knowing that you're on someone's radar screen.

If you are coming to Slovakia to teach, be sure to bring your original diplomas and teaching certificates. For any kind of employment it's also a good idea to bring an original copy of your birth certificate. An employer may need to see these documents or have them officially copied and translated for the work permit issued by the National Labor Office.

Some people can adapt easier to new surroundings than others, but everyone can get frustrated or feel out of place from time to time, particularly when upsetting things happen. When you aren't familiar with the customs, it's easy to get frustrated at another's seeming lack of respect: "I don't understand it. I refused an offer for a drink and still he keeps asking me to have one. Didn't he hear me the first time? These people are so pushy!" Remember that part of your education is to learn to decipher foreign customs and try not to let the differences annoy you.

You might find that many non-native English speakers are uncomfortable speaking to you in English, particularly in social settings, because they so strongly sense their language inadequacies. It's to your advantage to go out of your way to break through that barrier and work on making friends. For some, this is often easier said that done, but friendships are important in helping you get over culture shock and to learn about Slovak life. In addition, friends lead you to meeting new friends—always a good thing.

The number of expats living in Slovakia isn't as large as in the Czech Republic or Austria, but the network is extensive. For example, a Slovak acquaintance of yours knows a Canadian teaching English who goes regularly to a pub where he meets up with other English speakers. In your normal course of making contacts and meeting new people you will be introduced to expats sooner or later, but try to avoid the pitfall of becoming so involved with an expat group that you miss out on learning and experiencing your new culture.

There is still a disparity in the cost of living in, say, North America versus a former communist country, such as Slovakia or Poland. Groceries will cost you significantly less than they would at home. That goes for rent and transportation as well (though possibly not in big cities). Similarly, if you are working for a Slovak school or company and are paid a Slovak salary, it will be significantly less than what you would expect to make in your home country. Though it is much less, you will quickly learn that it is possible to survive on what you earn and can make it stretch to suit your needs. You've probably also figured out that you likely won't be amassing much savings either.

As I have heard it so eloquently stated, "You're not in Kansas, so don't act like it!" Keep an open mind and try not to fixate on how things are done back home in comparison to your adopted country. Not only does complaining not solve anything, it makes you a bitter and unpleasant person to be around and makes locals defensive and antagonistic.

Know what your purpose is for coming to Slovakia, and work on accomplishing your goals to the best of your ability and with professionalism. Using living abroad as a means to escape from something back home is not going to hold you up through the challenges that living in a new culture and environment brings.

Pay attention to your body and know your limits with food and alcohol. Be open to new experiences but know when to politely (but firmly) decline the next round of drinks.

Keep active. This is particularly good advice if you are feeling symptoms of culture shock such as depression, extreme homesickness, or wanting to withdraw from people (and their culture) who are different from you. Join a fitness club, go sightseeing, or take a language class.

Know your limits. When you need a break from culture overload, take some time out for yourself: make yourself your favorite foods from home, watch a favorite movie or T.V. show.

Culture shock in itself shouldn't be considered as an entirely negative experience. Feeling symptoms of culture shock means that you are sensitive to differences from your own culture and have the capacity to gain deeper self-knowledge as well as to be enriched by another culture. This sensitivity provides an important opportunity for learning.

My very last words to keep in mind are that travel and living abroad are extraordinary opportunities for growth, self-knowledge, and life-long experience. Some people think that you need to be adventurous or willing to take risks to travel or live abroad. This was never my philosophy; you just need to have a little determination, do some planning, and be flexible. In return, the value gained from traveling and living abroad is impossible to measure. Not only do you gain insight and appreciation for other cultures, but time away from your own country often makes you aware of who you are and the significance of where you come from.

Different generations of Slovak women

Facts at your Finger Tips: SLOVAKIA

Country name:	Conventional long form: Slovak Republic Conventional short form: Slovakia Local long form: *Slovenská republika* Local short form: *Slovensko* *Slovák*-Slovak (male), *Slovenka*-Slovak (female), *Slováci*-Slovaks.
Date of establishment:	January 1, 1993
National symbols:	\ \ \ \ \ \ \ National flag Coat of Arms
Official language:	Slovak
Capital city:	Bratislava (population approx. 450,000)
Neighboring Countries:	Austria, Czech Republic, Poland, Ukraine, Hungary
Area:	49,035 km2
Population:	5,379,455 (51.4% women)
Population density:	109/km2

Ethnicity of the population:	Slovak (85.8%), Hungarian (9.7%), Roma (1.7%), Czech (0.8%), Rusyn, Ukrainian, Russian, German, Polish and others (2%)
Population by religion:	Roman Catholic (68.9%), Protestant (6.9%), Greek Catholic (4.1%), Reform Christian (2%), undetermined (2.2%), atheist (13.7%)
State Organization:	Republic
Political system:	Parliamentary Democracy
Constitutional system:	Constitutional and legislative power (National Council of the Slovak Republic (SR)), executive power (president of the SR and government of the SR), judiciary power (constitutional court and courts)
President of the Republic:	Doc. JUDr. Ivan Gašparovič, CSc., Dr.h.c.
Prime Minister:	Doc. JUDr. Robert Fico, CSc.
Main political parties represented in the National Council:	Smer, Slovak Democratic and Christian Union (SDKÚ), Slovak National Party (SNS), Hungarian Coalition Party (SMK), Movement for a Democratic Slovakia (HZDS), Christian Democratic Movement (KDH)
Currency:	Slovak crown, 1 Skk = 100 haliers.
Exchange rate: (As of May 1, 2007)	Since March 19, 2007, the central rate of the Slovak crown is set at 35.4424 Skk to 1 euro. The crown is allowed to trade 15% above or below. Slovakia is expected to adopt the euro currency in 2009. 24.782 Skk = 1USD

© The Slovak Republic Government Office 1998-2007

Appendix B

Resource Guide

The following is a list of books and resources that I have found to be very informative. I have also noted the best place to purchase them, as some are more difficult to find than others.

Lorinc, John M. and Sylvia, *Slovak-English, English-Slovak Dictionary and Phrasebook.* ISBN 0-7818-0663-1

This is a very small "pocket-size" book that has the most comprehensive list of useful phrases and words that you will ever find. This little book is really a gem and is available through Amazon.

Böhmerová, Ada. *Slovak for You. Slovak for Speakers of English – Textbook for Beginners.* ISBN 0-86516-331-6 (US); ISBN 80-8046-106-6 (SK)

This is a Slovak language course book written for English language speakers. The format and structure of the lessons make it very easy to follow along, and the explanations are clear. The dialogues at the beginning of the chapters are useful. The most recent edition is light blue in color and most Slovak book stores carry it. It is also available through Amazon.

Orwell, Joseph P. *Vyše 1300 anglických slovíčok.*
ISBN 80-88980-06-2

This is a small red illustrated picture dictionary created for Slovak children who are starting to learn English. The great thing about it is that there are pictures of words in alphabetical order written in both English and Slovak. You might think it's silly to study Slovak from a children's book, but the illustrations are charming and might help you to memorize the words more easily. Most larger book stores in Slovakia carry it.

Škvareninová, Oľga. *Obrázkový Slovník Slovenčiny.*
ISBN 80-08-00913-6

This is another illustrated picture "dictionary." This book is unique because it contains ink illustrations of a range of subjects from plants and animals to occupations and types of sports. A number is assigned to each illustration that corresponds to a numbered list below it. This book is a great tool for getting familiar with vocabulary by associating words in specific groups. The book cover is orange in color but is more difficult to find in bookstores.

Slovakia - Walking Through Centuries of Cities and Towns
ISBN 80-07-01134-X

This is something like a picture book, guide book, and history book of the major cities and towns in Slovakia all rolled into one. It can be very useful when you are planning to travel around Slovakia and want to know which towns interest you for visiting in the future.

The Slovak Spectator, Spectacular Slovakia

This is a travel magazine published once a year by the Slovak Spectator. It's an incredibly useful guide because it is updated every year with the most recent information and has great articles about things to see and do around Slovakia. Articles in this issue discuss food, lodging, towns and regions of Slovakia, and history. Outside of Slovakia, you can purchase *Spectacular Slovakia* through *The Slovak Spectator* Web page; otherwise, it can be found at major news agents that sell *The Slovak Spectator* newspaper.

Quarterly newsletter *Slovakia*, Editor Helene Cincebeaux

The *Slovakia* newsletter provides articles and information on Slovak people, history, culture, traditions, and genealogy. It has been published for the past 20 years by the Slovak Heritage & Folklore Society International, www.helenezx.homestead.com or helenezx@aol.com

Appendix C

Useful Words and Phrases in Slovak

Though there are many rules in Slovak phonetics, below covers only the basics:

When looking at the Slovak language, the first thing you might notice over some of the letters is an inverted caret which looks like this ˇ. The function of this symbol is to 'soften' the sound of the letter. Most notably it changes the sound in the letters *c, s* and *z*.

> č = the sound like *ch* as in *ch*urch: *mačka* = cat
>
> š = the sound like *sh* as in *sh*ow: *šalát* = salad
>
> ž = the sound like *s* in vision: *môžem* = I can

It's also possible to have this symbol over or after a *d, l, n,* or *t,* but often the symbol looks more like an apostrophe than a caret. With these words, imagine that you are adding a *y* sound after those letters, for example pronouncing the word *new* like *nyew.*

> *ďakujem* ('dya-ku-yem) = thank you
>
> *marhuľa* ('mar-hool-ya) = apricot
>
> *deň* (dyen) = day

Vowel sounds are pronounced like vowels in a Romance language as Spanish or Italian, and an accent mark over a vowel extends the sound.

> *víno* (vee-no) = wine

The letter *j* has a sound like an English *y*.

> *ďakujem* ('dya-ku-yem) = thank you

The letter *c* is pronounced as *ts.*

> *cesnak* (tses-nak) = garlic

The letter *ä* sounds like the *e* in *pet.*

The letters *ch* are pronounced almost as a heavy *h* sound, much like the German pronunciation of *ch* like *Bach.*

General Words and Expressions

yes	*áno*
no	*nie*
good morning	*dobré ráno*
good day (hello-formal)	*dobrý deň*
good evening	*dobrý večer*
good night	*dobrú noc*
goodbye	*dovidenia*
hi (informal)	*ahoj, servus, čau*
how are you?	*ako sa máš?*
good, thanks.	*ďakujem, dobre.*
welcome!	*vitajte!*
thank you	*ďakujem*
you're welcome	*prosím*
please	*prosím*
excuse me	*prepáčte*
bon appetite!	*dobrú chuť!*
good!	*dobre!*
ok	*dobre*
I can't	*nemôžem*
I don't understand	*nerozumiem*
I want	*chcem*
to eat	*jesť*
to drink	*piť*
to sleep	*spať*
today	*dnes*
tomorrow	*zajtra*
yesterday	*včera*
now	*teraz*
later	*neskôr*

Questions

What is that?	*Čo je to?*
Where is/are?	*Kde je/sú?*
Where to?	*Kam?*
How far?	*Ako ďaleko?*
When?	*Kedy?*
Which one?	*Ktorý?*
How much?	*Koľko?*
Who is that?	*Kto je to?*
Do you speak English?	*Hovoríte po anglicky?*
Slowly, please.	*Pomaly, prosím.*
What does this mean?	*Čo to znamená?*
What's your name?	*Ako sa voláte?*
My name is	*Volám sa*

Signs

No smoking	*Nefajčiť*
Attention, Caution!	*Pozor!*
Entrance/ Exit	*Vchod/ Východ*
Toilets	*Toalety, WC (ve-tse)*
Men	*Muži*
Women	*Ženy, Dámy*
Open/ Closed	*Otvorené/ Zatvorené*
Arrivals/ Departures	*Príchod/ Odchod*
ambulance	*sanitka*
hospital	*nemocnica*
doctor	*lekár(ka)*
pharmacy	*lekáreň*
bank	*banka*
exchange	*zmenáreň*
police	*polícia*
restaurant	*reštaurácia*

Signs (continued)

café	*kaviareň*
store	*obchod*
grocery store	*potraviny*

Days of the Week

(The week starts on a Monday)

Monday	*pondelok*
Tuesday	*utorok*
Wednesday	*streda*
Thursday	*štvrtok*
Friday	*piatok*
Saturday	*sobota*
Sunday	*nedeľa*
day	*deň*
week	*týždeň*
month	*mesiac*
year	*rok*

Numbers

0	*nula*	11	*jedenásť*
1	*jeden*	12	*dvanásť*
2	*dva*	20	*dvadsať*
3	*tri*	30	*tridsať*
4	*štyri*	50	*päťdesiat*
5	*päť*	100	*sto*
6	*šesť*	200	*dvesto*
7	*sedem*	500	*päťsto*
8	*osem*	1,000	*tisíc*
9	*deväť*	5,000	*päť tisíc*
10	*desať*		

Various Foods / Drinks

bread	*chlieb*
water	*voda*
milk	*mlieko*
cheese	*syr*
butter	*maslo*
eggs	*vajcia*
meat	*mäso*
chicken	*kura/kuracie*
fish	*ryba*
beef	*hovädzie*
pork	*bravčové*
ham	*šunka*
rice	*ryža*
potatoes	*zemiaky*
fruit	*ovocie*
vegetables	*zelenina*
beer	*pivo*
wine	*víno*
juice	*džús*
coffee	*káva*
tea	*čaj*
salt	*soľ*
pepper	*čierne korenie*

APPENDIX D

CONVERSIONS AND MEASUREMENTS

Miles to Kilometers		Kilometers to Miles	
mi	km	km	mi
1	1.609	1	0.621
2	3.219	2	1.243
3	4.828	3	1.846
4	6.437	4	2.485
5	8.047	5	3.107
6	9.656	6	3.725
7	11.265	7	4.350
8	12.875	8	4.971
9	14.484	9	5.592
10	16.093	10	6.214
20	32.187	20	12.427
30	48.280	30	18.641
40	64.374	40	24.855
50	80.467	50	31.069
60	96.561	60	37.282
70	112.654	70	43.496
80	128.748	80	49.710
90	144.841	90	55.923
100	160.93	100	62.14

Feet (Inches) to Centimeters	
ft (in)	cm
1'0" (12)	30.5
2'0" (24)	61.0
3'0" (36)	91.4
4'0" (48)	121.9
5'0" (60)	152.4
5'1" (61)	154.9
5'2" (62)	157.5
5'3" (63)	160.0
5'4" (64)	162.6
5'5" (65)	165.1
5'6" (66)	167.6
5'7" (67)	170.2
5'8" (68)	172.7
5'9" (69)	175.3
5'10" (70)	177.8
5'11" (71)	180.3
6'0" (72)	182.9
6'1" (73)	185.4
6'2" (74)	188.0
6'3" (75)	190.5
6'4" (76)	193.0
6'5" (77)	195.6

Celsius and Fahrenheit					
C	F	C	F	C	F
-15	5.0	5	41.0	25	77.0
-14	6.8	6	42.8	26	78.8
-13	8.6	7	44.6	27	80.6
-12	10.4	8	46.4	28	82.4
-11	12.2	9	48.2	29	84.2
-10	14.0	10	50.0	30	86.0
-9	15.8	11	51.8	31	87.8
-8	17.6	12	53.6	32	89.6
-7	19.4	13	55.4	33	91.4
-6	21.2	14	57.2	34	93.2
-5	23.0	15	59.0	35	95.0
-4	24.8	16	60.8	36	96.8
-3	26.6	17	62.6	37	98.6
-2	28.4	18	64.4	38	100.4
-1	30.2	19	66.2	38.5	101.3
0	32.0	20	68.0	39	102.2
1	33.8	21	69.8	39.5	103.1
2	35.6	22	71.6	40	104.0
3	37.4	23	73.4	41	105.8
4	39.2	24	75.2	42	107.6

Pounds to Kilograms		Kilograms to Pounds	
lb.	kg	kg	lb.
1	0.454	1	2.205
2	0.907	2	4.409
3	1.361	3	6.614
4	1.814	4	8.818
5	2.268	5	11.023
6	2.722	6	13.228
7	3.175	7	15.432
8	3.629	8	17.637
9	4.082	9	19.842
10	4.536	10	22.046
20	9.072	20	44.092
30	13.608	30	66.139
40	18.144	40	88.185
50	22.68	50	110.231
60	27.216	60	132.277
70	31.751	70	154.324
80	36.287	80	176.37
90	40.823	90	198.416
100	45.359	100	220.46

CONVERSION CHART
FOR COOKING AND BAKING

For the purposes of rounding measurements, some conversions are approximate values.

VOLUME MEASUREMENTS (DRY)

⅛ teaspoon = 0.5 ml
¼ teaspoon = 1 ml
½ teaspoon = 2 ml
¾ teaspoon = 4 ml
1 teaspoon = 5 ml
1 tablespoon = 15 ml
¼ cup = 60 ml
⅓ cup = 75 ml
½ cup = 125 ml
⅔ cup = 150 ml
¾ cup = 175 ml
1 cup = 250 ml
2 cups = 1 pint = 500 ml
3 cups = 750 ml
4 cups = 1 quart = 1 L

VOLUME MEASUREMENTS (FLUID)

1 fluid oz (2 tablespoons) = 30 ml
4 fluid oz (½ cup) = 125 ml
8 fluid oz (1 cup) = 250 ml
12 fluid oz (1½ cups) = 375 ml
16 fluid oz (2 cups) = 500 ml

WEIGHT (MASS)

½ ounce = 15 g
1 ounce = 30 g
4 ounces = 120 g
8 ounces = 225 g
10 ounces = 285 g
12 ounces = 360 g
16 ounces = 1 pound = 450 g

DIMENSIONS

⅛ inch = 3 mm
¼ inch = 6 mm
½ inch = 1.5 cm
¾ inch = 2 cm
1 inch = 2.5 cm

OVEN TEMPERATURES

250ºF = 120ºC
275ºF = 140ºC
300ºF = 150ºC
325ºF = 160ºC
350ºF = 180ºC
375ºF = 190ºC
400ºF = 200ºC
425ºF = 220ºC
450ºF = 220ºC

BAKING PAN SIZES			
UTENSIL	SIZE IN INCHES/ QUARTS	METRIC VOLUME	SIZE IN CENTIMETERS
Baking or cake pan (square or rectangular)	8x8x2	2 L	20x20x5
	9x9x2	2.5 L	22x22x5
	12x8x2	3 L	30x20x5
	13x19x2	3.5 L	33x23x5
Loaf pan	8x4x3	1.5 L	20x10x7
	9x5x3	2 L	23x13x7
Round layer cake pan	8x1½	1.2 L	20x4
	9x1½	1.5 L	23x4
Pie plate	8x1¼	750 ml	20x3
	9x1¼	1 L	23x3
Baking dish or casserole	1 quart	1 L	-
	1½ quart	1.5 L	-
	2 quarts	2 L	-

Appendix E: Calendar of Name-days

	January		February		March
1	-	1	Tatiana, Táňa	1	Albín
2	Alexandra, Kasandra, Sandra	2	Erik, Erika	2	Anežka
3	Daniela, Genovéva	3	Blažej	3	Bohumil, Bohumila
4	Drahoslav, León	4	Veronika, Verona	4	Kazimír
5	Andrea, Artúr	5	Agáta	5	Fridrich, Friderika
6	Antónia	6	Dorota	6	Radoslav, Felícia
7	Bohuslava, Luciána	7	Vanda	7	Tomáš
8	Severín	8	Zoja	8	Alan, Alana
9	Alex, Alexej	9	Zdenko	9	Františka
10	Dáša	10	Gabriela	10	Branislav, Bruno
11	Malvína	11	Dezider	11	Angela, Angelika
12	Ernest	12	Ronald, Perla	12	Gregor, Gregoria
13	Rastislav	13	Arpád, Jordán	13	Vlastimil, Kira
14	Radovan	14	Valentín	14	Matilda
15	Dobroslav	15	Pravoslav, Georgína	15	Svetlana
16	Kristína	16	Ida, Liana	16	Boleslav, Amos
17	Nataša	17	Miloslava	17	Ľubica
18	Bohdana	18	Jaromír, Simeon	18	Eduard, Salvátor
19	Sára, Mário	19	Vlasta, Kurt	19	Jozef, Sibyla
20	Dalibor, Sebastián	20	Lívia, Alma	20	Víťazoslav, Klaudius,
21	Vincent	21	Eleonóra	21	Blahoslav
22	Zora, Auróra, Cyntia	22	Etela	22	Beňadik, Oktávia
23	Miloš, Selma	23	Roman, Romana	23	Adrián
24	Timotej	24	Matej, Jazmína	24	Gabriel
25	Gejza, Saul	25	Frederik, Frederika	25	Marián, Irisa
26	Tamara	26	Viktor	26	Emanuel
27	Bohuš	27	Alexander	27	Alena, Rupert
28	Alfonz, Manfréd	28	Zlatica	28	Soňa
29	Gašpar	29	Radomír	29	Miroslav
30	Ema			30	Vieroslava
31	Emil, Emiliána			31	Benjamín

	April		May		June
1	Hugo	1	Pamela, Amarila	1	Žaneta
2	Zita, Áron	2	Žigmund, Aténa	2	Xénia, Oxana
3	Richard	3	Galina, Horác	3	Karolína, Kevin
4	Izidor	4	Florián	4	Lenka, Lena
5	Miroslava, Mira	5	Lesana	5	Laura, Dorotej
6	Irena, Celestín	6	Hermína, Frída	6	Norbert, Norman
7	Zoltán, Armand	7	Monika, Mona	7	Róbert, Robin
8	Albert, Alberta	8	Ingrida	8	Medard
9	Milena, Erhard	9	Roland, Rolanda	9	Stanislava
10	Igor, Ezechiel	10	Viktória, Beatrica	10	Margaréta
11	Július, Leo, Ariela	11	Blažena, Miranda	11	Dobroslava, Flóra
12	Estera	12	Pankrác	12	Zlatko
13	Aleš, Norma	13	Servác	13	Anton, Tobiáš
14	Justína, Justín	14	Bonifác	14	Vasil, Bazil
15	Fedor, Fedora	15	Žofia, Brenda	15	Vít
16	Dana, Danica	16	Svetozár	16	Blanka, Bianka
17	Rudolf, Ralf	17	Gizela	17	Adolf, Adolfína
18	Valér	18	Viola	18	Vratislav, Sedrik
19	Jela	19	Gertrúda	19	Alfréd, Leonid
20	Marcel	20	Bernard, Bernadeta	20	Valéria, Florencia
21	Ervín	21	Zina, Teobald	21	Alojz, Elvis, Lejla
22	Slavomír, Jelena	22	Júlia, Juliána	22	Paulína
23	Vojtech, Roger	23	Želmíra	23	Sidónia
24	Juraj, Georg	24	Ela	24	Ján, Sean
25	Marek, Markus	25	Urban, Vanesa	25	Tadeáš,Olívia,
26	Jaroslava	26	Dušan	26	Adriána
27	Jaroslav, Aristid	27	Iveta	27	Ladislav, Ladislava,
28	Jarmila, Prudencia	28	Viliam, Elektra	28	Beáta, Bea
29	Lea	29	Vilma, Maxim	29	Peter, Pavol, Petra
30	Anastázia, Nastasia	30	Ferdinand	30	Melánia
		31	Petronela, Petrana		

July		August		September	
1	Diana, Tabita	1	Božidara, Penelopa	1	Drahoslava
2	Berta	2	Gustáv	2	Linda, Melinda, Rebeka
3	Miloslav	3	Jerguš, Nikodém	3	Belo
4	Prokop	4	Dominik, Dominika	4	Rozália, Róza
5	Cyril, Metod	5	Hortenzia	5	Regína, Justinián, Larisa
6	Patrik, Patrícia	6	Jozefína	6	Alica, Brian
7	Oliver, Donald	7	Štefánia	7	Marianna
8	Ivan, Kilián	8	Oskár, Virgínia	8	Miriama
9	Lujza	9	Ľubomíra	9	Martina, Gordon
10	Amália	10	Vavrinec, Laurenc	10	Oleg,
11	Milota	11	Zuzana	11	Bystrík, Helga
12	Nina	12	Darina, Dárius	12	Mária, Mariela, Marlena
13	Margita	13	Ľubomír, Belinda	13	Ctibor
14	Kamil	14	Mojmír,	14	Ľudomil, Serena
15	Henrich, Šarlota	15	Marcela	15	Jolana, Melisa
16	Drahomír, Karmen,	16	Leonard, Joachim	16	Ľudmila
17	Bohuslav	17	Milica, Mirón, Hyacinta	17	Olympia
18	Kamila	18	Elena, Helena	18	Eugénia, Ariadna
19	Dušana	19	Lýdia	19	Konštantín
20	Ilja, Eliáš, Eliána	20	Anabela, Arabela	20	Ľuboslav, Ľuboslava
21	Daniel	21	Jana, Johana	21	Matúš, Mirela
22	Magdaléna	22	Tichomír, Sigfríd	22	Móric
23	Oľga	23	Filip	23	Zdenka
24	Vladimír	24	Bartolomej	24	Ľuboš, Ľubor
25	Jakub, Žakelína	25	Ľudovít, Ludvig	25	Vladislav
26	Anna, Hana, Anita	26	Samuel	26	Edita
27	Božena	27	Silvia	27	Cyprián, Mirabela
28	Krištof	28	Augustín, August	28	Václav
29	Marta	29	Nikola, Nikolaj	29	Michal, Michaela
30	Libuša, Rowena	30	Ružena	30	Jarolím, Ráchel,
31	Ignác, Ignácia	31	Nora, Ramón, Ramona		

	October		November		December
1	Arnold, Belina	1	Denis, Denisa	1	Edmund
2	Levoslav	2	Cézar	2	Bibiána, Viviána
3	Stela	3	Hubert	3	Oldrich, Xavér
4	František, Edvin	4	Karol, Jesika	4	Barbora
5	Viera	5	Imrich	5	Oto, Geraldína
6	Natália	6	Renáta	6	Mikuláš, Nikolas
7	Eliška	7	René	7	Ambróz
8	Brigita	8	Bohumír	8	Marína
9	Dionýz	9	Teodor, Teodora	9	Izabela
10	Slavomíra	10	Tibor	10	Radúz, Herbert
11	Valentína, Selena	11	Martin, Maroš	11	Hilda
12	Maximilián	12	Svätopluk, Astrid	12	Otília
13	Koloman, Edgar	13	Stanislav	13	Lucia, Rosana, Roxana
14	Boris, Kalista	14	Irma	14	Branislava, Bronislava
15	Terézia, Tereza	15	Leopold	15	Ivica
16	Vladimíra	16	Agnesa	16	Albína
17	Hedviga	17	Klaudia	17	Kornélia
18	Lukáš	18	Eugen	18	Sláva, Graciána
19	Kristián	19	Alžbeta, Elizabeta	19	Judita, Abrahám
20	Vendelín	20	Félix	20	Dagmara
21	Uršuľa	21	Elvíra	21	Bohdan
22	Sergej	22	Cecília	22	Adela
23	Aloyza	23	Klement	23	Nadežda
24	Kvetoslava, Harold	24	Emília	24	Adam, Eva
25	Aurel	25	Katarína, Katrina	25	-
26	Demeter, Amanda	26	Kornel, Valerián	26	Štefan
27	Sabína, Sabrina	27	Milan, Virgil	27	Filoména
28	Dobromila	28	Henrieta, Gerhard	28	Ivana, Ivona
29	Klára, Klarisa	29	Vratko	29	Milada, Jonatán, Natanel
30	Šimon, Simona	30	Andrej, Ondrej	30	Dávid
31	Aurélia			31	Silvester

ABOUT THE AUTHOR

Margarete Hurn has built up an extensive knowledge of the Slovak culture and way of living through many years of involvement with the Slovak community in Southern California, and as an instructor of English, including teaching at the Slovak Technical University in Bratislava.

She is an experienced traveler of Central Europe, having lived and worked in Slovakia and Austria for five years. She began her travels through the former Czechoslovakia at the age of 15, before the country had opened its borders with the fall of communism. Since that time she has seen first hand the political, economic, and social changes that have taken place.

Currently, Margarete lives in the San Francisco Bay Area where she works as a technical writer.

INDEX

Do you have comments or a question about a subject not covered in this book? Your feedback is valuable for improving and updating our next edition.

Comments to the author may be sent by e-mail through the publisher at comments@modra-publishing.com.

For more information, resources, and updates on this book, visit **www.fgslovakia.com**.